# 50 Skills

## The Entrepreneurs' Handbook

How to design, start, grow and
protect your business

## RAY SPOONER

*For my sons, Steve, Ben, Adam, Luke and Alex*

First published in Great Britain as a softback original in 2019

Copyright © Ray Spooner

The moral right of this author has been asserted.

Typeset in New Century Schoolbook LT Std

Editing, design, typesetting and publishing by UK Book Publishing

www.ukbookpublishing.com

ISBN: 978-1-912183-79-1

# 50 Skills

## The Entrepreneurs' Handbook

# CONTENTS

# FOREWORD

I was lucky enough to be introduced to business at an early age by my father. I learned how to design and build a business that would give my family and I an amazing life, and today, generally speaking, I do what I want, when I want, with who I want. I have freedom and money to enjoy it. Believe me, there is nothing like this feeling.

On the flip side, building a business has not been easy. On the contrary, I've had to work very hard to develop myself and I've had to sacrifice my social life and friends in favour of the business. On occasions working very long hours at the office and then at home, weekend after weekend in study. This intensity went on for at least twenty years. I can still remember hearing the sound of lawn mowers while I was hard-at-it, in my study under a little lamp. At times, it's been very stressful, but I wanted freedom, so I was willing to pay the price.

Throughout the book I've tried to give you an unbiased view of business, so you can decide whether it's for you. I understand not all people want the risks associated with running a business. Most people are happy working 9-5, with little or no responsibility. Most not even interested in advancing their careers, and that's fine – the world needs different types of people.

Generally speaking, I've found people who start businesses want more out of life, and they value their freedom. They believe that they can build a better future for their families by serving others, just as we benefit from our lifestyle today, created by those who served us in the past. If you are one of those people, this book is for you.

In this, my first book, I've relayed my long years of experience and business education, so that you can design and build the life you want, for you, your family and for the benefit of future generations.

I'd like to take this opportunity to thank you for investing money and time into my book. I've put months of my life into its writing, and I believe it can really help you improve your life.

Please get in touch through my website *www.carmelcresttraining.com/50skills* if there's anything I can help you with.

# ABOUT

This book is to help you become a successful entrepreneur. It's packed with information I've gained over thirty-five-years in business.

## 50 SKILLS WILL TEACH YOU HOW TO:

- ✓ Design your business.
- ✓ Start and grow your business.
- ✓ Protect your business.
- ✓ Master personal development techniques.
- ✓ Become a master-manager of people.
- ✓ Understand the essential financials.
- ✓ Succeed in business.

### WHO'S THE BOOK FOR?

This book will be invaluable to you if you are:

- ➤ Considering starting a business and want to learn from someone who has done it and had a good level of success.
- ➤ Wanting to professionalise or grow your current business.
- ➤ Interested in progressing your career in your current business.

> ➤ Interested in progressing your knowledge of business, personal development and managing others.

It includes 50 business topics that I've learned mainly through experience, and also through formal education and constant personal development over the years.

The book is an all-round business skills guide book. Written by a long-term business owner, who started at the bottom and has designed and built a life that has made him financially free.

I cover subjects I don't believe have been covered in one book before. They are all you'll need to start and build a business. I know this to be true, because they have worked for me, and others I mentor.

## WHY I WROTE THE BOOK

The idea for the book came from the mentoring I was doing with my sons and others, some of whom thought it would be a good idea to put the subjects I was teaching down in a book.

Also, having read many business books over the years, in an attempt to gain knowledge to grow my business, I felt there was a need for a book by a business owner that gives the real story of what it's like building a business from nothing, not dressing it up in any way.

Nothing I've said is my opinion, just the facts, based on my experience, good and bad. Dealing with different types of people and learning the hard way how to build a business.

In the many books I've read, I've felt some of the writers assume readers already have a good level of business knowledge. Business terminology is used with the assumption that people are familiar with the concepts. In my experience, many are not. Even business owners I come across don't know the difference between gross and net profit, or how to read a profit and loss account or a balance sheet. I find many have very little business knowledge at all. That's probably why a very high percentage of companies fail within the first five years.

I've tried to make no assumptions here; I've explained the meaning of every term before explaining the concept.

During my research, I struggled to find a book that gave the whole picture. Most cover one area of business such as finance or motivation. I've tried to give you the whole picture; I want you to be armed with everything you need to cope in the world of business. One reference book that covers everything.

Some subjects are not in great depth, and they are not intended to be. As an entrepreneur, you employ professionals to do the detail. But you certainly need a good general knowledge of everything so you can communicate effectively with your professional team.

One more reason I wrote the book. I'm frankly fed up with authors citing Steve Jobs, Warren Buffet, Elon Musk and the like, as outstanding examples of entrepreneurs, for young people to aspire to. Whilst they obviously are, there are 8.2 billion people on the planet, and of those, these three geniuses (and I mean that in the literal sense) are probably among the top ten business achievers in recent history. Trying to live up to that is a tall order, and in reality, it's not going to happen, or would you even want it to happen?

Steve Jobs died at age fifty-six, with a poor relationship with his daughter and turbulent relationships with colleagues. I'm willing to bet that anxiety played some part in his early death.

In reality, there are some pretty amazing business owners among the other 8.2 billion, who, to varying degrees, run great businesses, and have learned the formula to happiness, and have healthy, happy, wealthy and long lives.

Let's take the pressure away, aim for achievement, yes, but also a balanced, happy and prosperous life. That's what I've aimed to give you in this book.

## RESPONSIBILITY TO OTHERS

Another reason I decided to write the book, without meaning to sound soft, was because I'm at that stage in my career where I get as much satisfaction helping others, as I do achieving myself. I also feel it my responsibility to pass on the knowledge that has given my family and I such an amazing life.

## BECAUSE I WISH I'D HAD THIS INFORMATION WHEN I STARTED

I sincerely wish I'd had a chance to sit down for a few days with a successful business owner at the start of my career. I'm sure I'd have made fewer mistakes, and I'm sure my progress would have been quicker. The way I have spent my money over the years would certainly have been different. Thirty-five years of learning and successful business management are in this book, gems of wisdom, invaluable to new and existing business owners and managers.

50 Skills is packed with the kind of knowledge only someone who has run a business for most of their life could know, all the grey areas no college syllabus could ever teach.

## HOW 50 SKILLS IS STRUCTURED

There are six parts, plus a bonus section.

### Part 1. Why Start a Business?

I discuss my life as an employee compared to my later life as a business owner. In doing so, my hope is that you will understand the enormous benefits a life as an entrepreneur can bring. But also, the price you have to pay earlier in life, for that level of comfort later on.

### Part 2. Personal Development

We delve into personal development and people management, which underpins everything you do as an entrepreneur. This knowledge will give you the confidence to go forward into business and make you a wise leader. In my mind, this section is probably the most important in the book. With this skill-set, you will be poised to run a business in any sector.

### Part 3. Designing and Starting Your Business

This is about the hard business skills, generic to any business. We talk through how to get started, from your idea, to going live. I give you a template to design your business, write an organisation chart, job roles, processes and systems. Plus, lots of my experience of dealing with the minefield of different personality types, of people in different disciplines.

### Part 4. Growing Your Business

Now your business is up and running, I talk about how to grow your business including some economic concepts you need to understand before you start. This section will help you understand organic and driven growth, and where to target your sales and marketing effort.

### Part 5. Must Know Financials

An absolute must for any business owner for several reasons. To protect your business, you must have a good understanding of financial management. Also, you need to be able to speak 'the language of business' to be credible.

We discuss in easy-to-understand chunks, the essential financials, such as turnover, gross and net profit, budgeting, cash flow and other subjects you must know as an entrepreneur.

### Part 6. Why Businesses Go Wrong

The majority of new businesses fail; this is a fact. I don't want you to be one of them. I talk about the reasons why my business nearly went wrong, then I give you techniques to make sure you know how to protect yourself against them. If you learn the concepts I explain here, the chances of your business going under are very small indeed, I'd like to think near impossible.

### Bonus Section

I conclude with a bonus section I call Gathering of Wealth. It's not directly about business, more what you do with the money you make. Again, I wish someone had explained this to me when I started – I'd have been financially free much earlier.

So, let's get into the book and in the first section, Why start a business, I'll explain why I believe you should consider this as your way of life.

# PART 1:
## WHY START A BUSINESS

I took a train into London a few months ago during the rush hour. It was a rainy day and the train from Cambridge to London was packed at 8am. I didn't enjoy standing the one hour and twenty-minute journey.

As I looked around the train, lots of people were looking down at their devices; the ones I could see were watching films or playing games.

To me, train or car time is down time; down time is learning time. I'd brought my ear phones and a was listening to 24 Assets by Daniel Priestly. But then I realised, this was an indication of the very reason these people do this journey day after mind numbing day. Most are not interested in developing themselves, but are content with working for someone else, and sitting on a train for three hours a day, forty-eight weeks a year, year in year out.

As I stood there, I remembered why I wanted to run a business all those years ago. I reminded myself of the dislike I have for the whole 9-5 work ethic, and I thanked my lucky stars my dad asked me to join him in business and taught me the skills I needed to get started.

In the coming chapters I want to share with you the amazing benefits that are waiting for you if you start your own business, and also a few of the difficulties you'll need to overcome.

Let me first explain how my life used to be as an employee, then later as a business owner.

## LIFE AS AN EMPLOYEE

My first job aged sixteen was an apprentice toolmaker. It was a five-year City & Guilds apprenticeship, which I completed successfully, followed by two years working as a toolmaker. Toolmaking is a skilled profession, and I loved the detailed work. But apart from that and the money, which was very good, that was the only thing I liked.

We had to be at the factory at 7.50am to put on overalls and rub barrier cream into our hands. We were working with oils and many people used to get dermatitis. Then we clocked on at 8am. This meant physically sliding a card into a machine, to have the time stamped on it.

If you were more than a minute late, you would be docked fifteen minutes' pay. More than fifteen, docked thirty, more than thirty, an hour.

We clocked out at 12.00 for lunch, but not a moment before. Then back at 1pm and out at 5pm. Working Saturday mornings until 12.00 was compulsory. Most of the time in the summer, I got to mow the boss's lawn, which was my favourite part of the week, fresh air, ah.

There was a large clock over the factory doors, and some days an hour seemed like an entire morning. I hated it. The confinement, routine, control, the same people, the monotonous production tasks. I would have done, and eventually did, anything to get out of there. I used to watch the steel delivery lorries driving off, longing to be hiding away in the back, and out into the world.

I put up with this for seven long years. Then, when I was twenty-two, my father, who was a construction building manager, had been made redundant. He asked me if I'd be interested in starting up in business with him, as a builder's labourer. At that time, I was earning nearly £400 a week as a skilled toolmaker. A considerable amount of money for a lad of twenty-two. My father said that he could pay me £150 per week.

I learned something about myself that day, that money wasn't my main motivation in a job, because I'd have joined him for pocket money to get out of that place. I left, and in doing so, had wasted the previous seven years of my life to start at the bottom again in the building trade.

First lesson, think long and hard about your career. I had seven years of watered growth on my tree, then I pulled it out to plant another one.

## LIFE AS AN ENTREPRENEUR

Digging trenches was my first job, and I loved it, or rather I loved the open spaces, and the freedom. It wasn't long before I knew that the construction industry was for me. Looking back, it could have been any industry where I had more freedom, space to think for myself and the bosses weren't so hung up about times. The industry suited my non-conformist personality and there was plenty of scope for advancement.

My dad progressed the business quickly, and I progressed too. I persuaded him to give me a day off to go back to college and I also did night-school. I did an HNC, ONC, Degree, then finally Masters, which I didn't complete. I started a PhD too, but that kind of detail wasn't for me. I did eighteen straight years in education, including night school for much of that, after my five-year apprenticeship in toolmaking. I gave up a hell of a lot of my younger life to personal development and lost many friends in the process.

My father had a double hip replacement and retired eight years after starting the business, at aged fifty-five. The eight years he had been in business gave him enough money to retire. I still don't know how he did it. He mentored me to take over in the last year, leaving me a young managing director aged twenty-eight.

The firm had sales of more than £0.8m the year he left, and within five years we were turning over nearly £4m with good profits. We had computerised the business, had monthly management accounts, and written and implemented new management systems. The business was professionalising and booming.

I'd found my calling. I loved everything about it. I loved being the boss and I thrived on the pressure. I began to realise I was fairly good at it. I've never looked back.

## BENEFITS OF RUNNING YOUR OWN FIRM

There is no comparison between my life as an employee and my life as an entrepreneur; for all its worry and difficulties, I've loved every moment of my journey – well, not the anxiety bits, but I'll come to that.

As an employee, I had no freedom, but as a business owner, I had total freedom, and in my mind, no amount of money can buy that. Even if you do keep long hours, as a business owner you work when you want to, rather than when you have to work.

I want my sons and you to have the life you want, not what the boss wants for you. As the famous motivational speaker Jim Rohn says:

**"Guess what the boss has in mind for you? Not much."**

I was struggling to find the right words to describe my depth of feeling on this issue. So I asked my son Steve what he thought was the best thing about running a business. After a moment he replied, "the autonomy".

Autonomy, freedom from external control or influence. That's the single word that says it all. To me that means:

- ➤ Never having to ask the boss for time off to see your child's nativity.
- ➤ Designing the future you want, not the future the boss wants for you.
- ➤ Working the hours you want, not the hours your boss wants.
- ➤ Keeping the profits you make, not what the boss gives you.
- ➤ Opportunity to earn unlimited income.
- ➤ Plan your work around your family.
- ➤ Create a legacy.

I hope this chapter has given you food for thought, and if you decide to follow my path, in the coming chapters, I'm going to give you all the knowledge and skills you need to design, start, grow and stay in business. Including templates and spreadsheets I've prepared for you on the website that accompanies this book.

But before we get into the hard business skills. The next chapter, as I have said, is, I believe, the most important. It's all about you. Your personal skills and knowledge, and it gets pretty serious and deep sometimes, but then running a firm is serious and deep. The better you understand yourself, the better you'll understand others, and running a business is all about finding people, and encouraging them to want to work toward your vision.

# PART 2:
## PERSONAL DEVELOPMENT

# SKILL 1

## UNDERSTANDING WEALTH

Skill 1 sets the scene for the book. As I said in the introduction, to me life is about finding happiness, and happiness can only be found in a balanced life. So the advice I've given you in this book is not all about money and business, it brings in all other areas of your life, which enable you to be effective in business and bring in the money.

I'd like to introduce you to a very important concept, which it took me a while to learn. But when I did, it changed my priorities and life for the better. The concept of wealth.

I read somewhere that wealth is happiness. If that's true, wealth must be more than just money, because I've realised money alone doesn't make me happy.

I've learned that it is impossible for me to be happy without several components being present. First, my main relationships must be solid, my children and partner. Then my health must be good, which means I'm eating well and exercising. Also, I must have no money worries. When I have all this, I'm very happy.

I learned this the hard way, after my divorce in fact. Before then I was a workaholic, obsessed with building my business. Which probably resulted, in part, to the breakup of my marriage, followed by my firm suffering massively as a result.

I eventually learned that true wealth, hence happiness, can only be achieved with a balance of three things:

- ➢ Relationships
- ➢ Health
- ➢ Money

## RELATIONSHIPS

I have a wonderful relationship with my children, their children and my partner, that I nurture and prioritise over everything. Basically, I give them time, and that tells them that they are important to me. Indirectly, this is very important to my business. When my relationship with my children, grandchildren and partner is good, I feel content and I have a strong purpose, which drives me forward in my business.

I didn't realise that in the early days. I neglected home life for work, and as a result, it all fell apart.

## HEALTH

I ate anything in those early years, but mostly pizza, especially when I stayed late at work, which was most of the time. Luckily, I always exercised to an extent. Now I'm very aware of eating good clean food and exercising to stay young and healthy, so I can work hard, lead an active and hopefully long life and look good for my partner.

## MONEY

With the support of strong relationships and energy from good health, I am able to go out and build my businesses, and earn money to enjoy a good life. It's all in balance.

When you give equal priority to all three components, it becomes self-fulfilling, a positive cycle of achievement and happiness. One feeds the other. It's amazing and it makes me very happy indeed. It gives me a strong purpose in life, because I want this life to continue.

That, to me, is true wealth, and that's what I want to pass on to you in this book.

# SKILL 2

## THE CONSCIOUS AND UNCONSCIOUS MIND

I put this section in because I've found it very useful to have an understanding of how I, and all humans, learn and retain information. I don't want you forgetting what you read here, do I?!

The best model I could find to explain the concept is by Sigmund Freud, called the 'topographical model of the mind', which explains his idea of the way the mind is structured. I have found this to be true for me.

The model, representing the brain, is presented as an iceberg, with three levels.

> ➤ The unconscious mind – This is the bottom layer representing 95% of your behaviours. You have no control of this part of your mind.
> ➤ The preconscious mind – The middle brain. You have partial control, such as recall of telephone numbers, techniques, and skills.
> ➤ The conscious mind – The top layer, under our complete control, such as what you are currently thinking, representing only 5% of our behaviours.

## UNCONSCIOUS MIND

I first became interested in this subject when I lost our company a few million pounds, maybe more, many years ago. At that time, I had no idea that we have no control of 95% of our behaviour.

I was at a meeting with an architect who had a reputation for being aggressive. He sure lived up to his reputation – he was horrible, belittling me in front of the client. Now my natural reaction to this treatment is to bite back, which I did. My father was aggressive in his younger days, and I think I learned my behaviour from him.

In the moment, I forgot that his firm gave mine a lot of work. But it felt good to put this bully in his place, for a moment anyway. But that was quickly replaced with a feeling of, oh shit, what have I done, when I realised we would we lose the project, and all future projects, probably millions of pounds over the years.

It was at this point I realised that I needed to understand how to control my emotions. This meant learning how my unconscious mind worked, since it controls 95% of our behaviours.

I learned we are all pre-programmed with instincts and unconscious behaviours at birth, passed down from our parents, and we've added more habits as we've gone through life. All this dictates our actions and behaviours, and forms our personality.

This is both useful – for example, when your instinct is to fight or flight from danger – but possibly not so useful when you react in anger in a business meeting.

To get into the long-term unconscious memory, an event has to be either extreme, as in a traumatic experience, or possibly a highly pleasurable experience – we all remember our first love, do we not? Or more often, it enters through repetition.

It is unclear whether it is possible to control your unconscious mind by being consciously aware of your actions and emotions, but in my experience, training in the subject you are trying to control, such as anger management, can definitely help bring your unconscious actions to your conscious mind. Today I am definitely more aware of my unconscious behaviours, and try to keep them well under control, but it does take effort.

## PRE-CONSCIOUS MIND

Freud implies the pre-conscious is somewhere between complete consciousness and unconscious, and in this area of the brain, skills can be recalled easily and used at will, like an old phone number you had and remember many years after you stop using it.

This has definitely been my experience; for example, when I am presenting a subject I know well, I can recall the details easily. Although the knowledge has become part of me, it's not so far in my unconscious that I cannot recall it at will, like say a memory from twenty years ago that is deep in the unconscious.

I hope you will practise the skills you learn in this book often – as they say, repetition, repetition, repetition, will plant the knowledge firmly in the pre-conscious mind, to be recalled by you at will. The skills will become part of you. But as the other saying goes, if you don't use it, you lose it.

Once this new knowledge becomes part of who you are, you will have in effect become more than you were before, you will have developed as a person, and remember, the only way to have more, is to become more.

# SKILL 3

## BECOME MORE TO HAVE MORE

I love this concept, and again, it sets the scene for this book. There is a brilliant concept that says, nothing in your life will change, until you change. It's obvious really, at least when it's pointed out to you.

I have personally experienced this. I mentioned earlier that I spent much of my life in education and personal development. What I didn't realise at the time was as I learned more and became more, I got more. It just seemed to happen. As my knowledge grew, so did my wealth.

Now, many years on, I am sure that there is only one way you can ever get more in this world: you have to become more than you are now. People that develop themselves become more and have more.

I'd like you to take a moment to read and re-read the following words by the famous Jim Rohn. They are probably among the most important I've ever read. If I gave you this book and it only had these two lines, and you understood the meaning, then that would be worth hundreds of thousands, maybe millions to you and your family.

"You can have more than you've got, because
you can become more than you are."

**Jim Rohn**

The only way to improve any area of your life is to improve yourself first. There is no other way. Sorry for the repetition, but I want you to get this point.

The problem with not developing yourself, as my old NLP coach used to say, is that:

"If you always do what you've always done,
you'll always get what you've always got".

If you're happy with what you've got, that's fine, but if you're looking for more, then there is no other way than to develop yourself.

I've found on occasions, even with my own sons, some people resist education, and as my dad used to say. "you can take a horse to water, but you can't make it drink"; how true.

Please don't be that short-sighted person. Fulfil all you can be, embrace learning, develop yourself, and I promise your life will change for the better. It will have to, because you'll be better.

## LEARNING METHODS

Technology has made a massive difference to how you can learn; there is so much material at your disposal. There really is no excuse for anyone not to develop themselves. Here are some of the ways that I learn:

- ➢ Audio Books (on the go)
- ➢ Books
- ➢ YouTube
- ➢ The internet
- ➢ Short courses
- ➢ Mentoring

Technology has made a massive difference to when you can learn too:

- ➢ In the car
- ➢ On the train
- ➢ In the gym
- ➢ Walking
- ➢ Ironing
- ➢ Cooking

Fill your down-time with content – the hours you can win back are incredible. Take my old car journey to the office.

For many years my journey was an hour there and back five days a week. I did this for approximately forty-six weeks of the year.

That's ten hours a week, times forty-six weeks. That's four hundred and sixty hours, and that's eleven and a half work weeks.

Just imagine what you can learn from audio books in over two months, and that's only from driving. If you listen in the gym, walking the dog, cooking etc, your speed of development would be incredible.

I know this to be absolutely the case. My sons are products of this type of learning, as am I.

My sixteen year old son Alex has learned to buy multiple properties in the nine months since he left school. Dealing with viewings, legal paperwork, mortgage brokers, estate agents and solicitors. He even negotiates with letting agents and manages the entire letting process.

He has listened to all he can find on the subject and attended many short courses. With guidance from me and other colleagues, his progress has been astonishing. All this has taken him approximately nine months to achieve, and he's not even old enough to drive. By the age of twenty-two, when most are leaving university, he'll own at least two properties.

My twenty-one-year-old son Luke is a bookkeeper. He trains other bookkeepers in our company and is now on a fast-track two-year mentoring programme to be a financial director. He already has his first buy-to-let property, which he self manages, paid for from the savings he has earned from the age of sixteen. This brings him in £500 a month for the rest of his life.

I don't tell you all this to boast about my sons, I tell because they are evidence of what can be achieved at such a young age, if only you would dedicate yourself to personal development, saving and investing.

Whatever age you are, you have a massive head start over previous generations whose main source of knowledge was the local library. It's here for you at the push of a button, so I do hope you choose to use it.

It's my hope that by the end of this section, you will believe that you can only have more, if you become more.

## THE GURUS

I owe much of my personal development knowledge to several gurus. It would be wrong of me not to give them credit here. The three that have had most influence on me are listed below. I hope you will seek out these teachers – they have books, audio books and plenty of material on YouTube. In no particular order:

➢ Jim Rohn
➢ Brian Tracey
➢ Robin Sharma

## BOOKS AND AUDIO BOOKS

Make the best habit of your life to immerse yourself in audio books every day. Listen to auto-biographies of all the greats, and as many personal development books as you can. Read general personal development and read industry specific books.

There are hundreds of books you should read, but my must-read list is as follows.

➢ Think and Grow Rich by Napoleon Hill
➢ The Richest Man in Babylon by George Clayton
➢ The E Myth by Michael Gerber
➢ The Slight Edge by Jeff Olson
➢ How to Win Friends and Influence People by Dale Carnegie

Many subsequent books have been based on Think and Grow Rich, which explains that you can have what you want in life if you focus on that thing, make plans and take action. This is the granddaddy of personal development books, in my opinion.

25

The Richest Man in Babylon is a story about how to handle money and become rich. Please read this and share it with your children at as early an age as possible. It will teach you how to deal with money and if you want, to get rich.

The E Myth is a must if you are a specialist in any particular field, and you are considering starting a business. It sets out that business skills are very different from technical skills. Michael Gerber coined the phrase "technician". It was instrumental in me setting systems in my business.

The Slight Edge philosophy makes us aware of the importance of the everyday little steps. It encourages us to take small daily routines and actions, creating a compound effect to deliver the lives we desire.

How to win Friends and Influence People by Dale Carnegie is thought to be the seminal sales book. It is amazing for anyone who will be customer facing including all entrepreneurs.

## PERSONAL DEVELOPMENT VS FURTHER EDUCATION

I have a dislike of the further education system, and this is why.

- ➢ The system trains you for a job. A lifetime exchanging your time for money, caught in the rat race. Whatever your income, if you stop working, you stop earning.
- ➢ Most of what I've achieved has been through personal development and through specific technical training relevant to my job.
- ➢ Many parents have been conditioned by the education system, to believe that if their child doesn't go to university, they are a failure. This is wrong.

> ➤ I've seen so many young people come out of university with a degree not knowing what they want to do, and with big debt.
> ➤ On many occasions, young people are wasting their time from age sixteen until twenty-two, when they could be using that time to build a career and earn money.
> ➤ It is the government's education system and not yours, their interests and not yours.
> ➤ The syllabus is so broad and most of it will not be relevant to you. It's designed for everyone, not you.
> ➤ After a few weeks in my company, most young graduates say they wished they had started work at sixteen.
> ➤ At the age of twenty-two, when most people are leaving university, my sons were running departments in my businesses and owned property.
> ➤ The education system does not suit all learning styles, and disadvantages practical learners, who make up the majority of the population.
> ➤ It lacks subjects that deal with self-awareness, life skills and people skills. Needed in all walks of life.

I'll leave my case against further education in the capable hands of Mehmet Umut Ermeç, and this piece from his website.

### "Elephant in the Room: Most Students and Educators Don't Like Our Education System

Most educators I know don't feel like students benefit from them enough. Most students I know don't think they benefit from their teachers enough. Most students I know don't like to sit passively in classrooms for hours. Most teachers I know don't like to repeat the same lectures again and again. Most students I know don't like to do homework. Most teachers I know don't like to grade homework at all. Most students I know favour hands-on training over spoken lessons. Most teachers I know prefer labs and workshops, which are rare, over classroom lectures, which are common. Most students I know would die for a flexible class schedule that can be customized, which is unheard of in our current system. Most teachers I know complain about the conflicts between their personal agendas and the school calendars all the time".

Mehmet Umut Ermeç, Educator/Entrepreneur closing the gap between what educational systems offer and employers demand.

## THE CASE FOR PERSONAL DEVELOPMENT

I have grown to love personal development. Here are the reasons why:

- ➢ The core of personal development is self-understanding. People must understand themselves, in order to help or manage others and achieve in any walk of life.
- ➢ Humans only achieve by cooperation, and personal development focusses on relationships and people skills, essential to life and any career.
- ➢ It teaches the benefits of goal setting and this is crucial to achievement in life and business.
- ➢ It encourages a good work ethic.
- ➢ The training you choose is completely relevant to your chosen career.
- ➢ You can learn at a time and style that suits you.

For the case for personal development, I leave you with this classic quote from the master Jim Rohn, that says it all.

"Formal education will make you a living; self-education will make you a fortune."

**Jim Rohn**

# SKILL 4

## THE STUDY OF HUMANS

Fairly early on, I realised my success in business was going to rely on my relationships, so logic told me to learn more about the psychology of people. I'm glad I did, because I'm sure it's this, more than the hard business skills, that has led to my success.

My reading led me to human psychology, which led me to Neuro Linguistic Programming (NLP), and then Anthropology (stay with me), which is the study of humans and human behaviour.

I'll give you a very small example of why I've found people skills more important than business skills.

Take accounts, for example. I knew nothing about accounts when I took over the business, I had to learn fast, and I did. But I can tell you this: learning accounts was the easy bit. Managing the personality of our bookkeeper was far more challenging, made worse because I was much younger than her.

First, I thought I'd get around this by recruiting people I got on with. But I soon realised people are very different in an interview, and also, I needed a lot of people. I had to learn to get along with all personality types, and to see things from their point of view.

This is why you need a good understanding of human psychology, to learn more about yourself, and in doing so, learn about others. I learned in NLP that we compare all new learning to ourselves first, then, as this becomes part of us, we automatically use what we've learned to help and manage others.

Andrew Carnegie, the famous steel baron of 19th century America, discussed in his autobiography that if he was going to be successful, it was not the study of the steel industry, but the study of men, that would make him his fortune, and it did.

I'd go as far as to say that your success as an entrepreneur will be in relation to the extent to which you can first understand and master yourself, then use that knowledge to manage others.


## NLP

NLP is a branch of psychology that studies the language of the mind, the way humans use the brain in communication. I hope you will seek out a good NLP course to further your knowledge.

NLP was extremely useful to me in understanding myself and others. I believe it has given me an advantage in business, and I feel empowered with the knowledge it has given me.

I remember during our training we learned several techniques, including body language and eye movements. This is basic NLP, but even this is very useful.

For example, I'd never considered that some people were naturally good at body language and some not. It never occurred to me that, like anything else, this is a learned skill that can be improved. I now understood why my six feet six-inch site manager was not liked by so many people. He tended to stand bolt upright, chest out. He was an intimidating figure to have standing in front of you, and many of the site personnel didn't give him the chance to get to know him as a person. I taught him to adjust slightly to shorter people, and be consciously aware of mirroring techniques.

We also learned that humans take in information through our senses, and this varies greatly from person to person. This is known as learning styles, and I now adapt my teaching style to suit the individual. If it's a group, I try to cover all the learning styles. This has been very helpful in my career, especially when I'm trying to convince my team of a particular course of action, and particularly useful for teachers of any kind.

Humans have an internal and external set of senses. Have you ever been presenting, and some of the class are looking down? Chances are they are having internal thoughts or feelings. If they are having an internal dialogue, it's very doubtful, near impossible, to focus on external voices. As a presenter you must stop, wait for them to look up, then when eye contact is re-established, talk again.

Eye movements are another example. You can generally tell the type of thought a person is having by their eye movements. If you ask a question that requires an answer from memory, for example, 'why did you leave your last job?', the eyes should move to the right as you face them, and they will be drawing from memory. Movement to the left is auditory construction, indicating they are constructing their reply, hence a lie could be being told. You have no idea of the details, just that a lie could be being told. This is useful in business and in life.

## ANTHROPOLOGY

The study of humans and human behaviour. There's an amazing book on this subject by Yuval Noah Harari, called Sapiens: A brief History of Humankind. It explains how human behaviour has evolved, from its pre-human origins. Of particular interest is biological anthropology, which deals with behavioural aspects of human beings.

I have found this knowledge incredibly helpful in business. If you have an understanding of our biology, how hormones affect our moods for example, you have a big advantage in the workplace. It will give you empathy and help you find win-win solutions and set-up win-win circumstances that will motivate staff towards your goal, whilst satisfying their unconscious instinctual need.

I wanted to draw your attention to these subjects, and to the fact that there is more to being an entrepreneur than just business knowledge; the more you understand how humans tick, the better you'll be with people and the more you'll achieve in business.

As well as being extremely interesting, a deeper knowledge of human behaviour will give you confidence, wisdom and power, an advantage over people with just technical training.

# SKILL 5

## INTEGRITY AND TRUST

Do what you say you are going to do

Why do people think they can pull the wool over the eyes of an experienced intelligent person?

A clever business person can smell BS a mile away, even the tiniest amount. The thing is, they will rarely contradict you, they'll just let you keep on spouting the BS to see how deep a hole you'll dig.

I've come across so many people in business, who say things like, "I'll email that to you tonight", or, "I'll get the quote back to you by Friday", or, "I'll call you tomorrow", but tomorrow never comes, or it comes a few days late.

These people don't seem to realise that people pick up on this instantly. Even one small slip like this could ruin your chances of working with a client. Why? Because it says everything about you and your values.

Please take my advice: in business, if you say you are going to do something, do it. If not, don't say you will. No one asked you to.

It's disrespectful and shows a lack of integrity and intelligence. I'd never consider working with a person who acted like that.

## WORK WITHIN THE LAW

I'd like to take this opportunity to get one thing clear. If you want to build a substantial business, there is only one way: honestly. Full stop. Pay your taxes, no envelopes, no under the counter deals, no cash, only open, honest business. That's if you want to build a professionally run, meaningful business. Anything else is just short sightedness.

## WORK WITHIN THE LAW NOT THE RULES

Work within the law at all times, but rules are open to interpretation. I do, in fact, encourage you to bend the rules every way you can to get what you want in business. So long as it's completely ethical and within the law. The reason I say this, is that some rules are so stupid they deserve to be got around.

For example, my company was once excluded from a tender list for painting a multi-storey car park, because we hadn't actually painted a car park before. We had painted hundreds of other types of buildings, but not a car park. Now we just say we've painted car parks and we get on tender lists. A stupid rule deserves a stupid response.

## FACING DIFFICULT SITUATIONS

Have you ever taken the easy option when faced with a difficult thing to do? I did, in the early days.

35

This is perfectly natural; humans have developed hormones designed to keep us away from danger, and towards safety. We avoid confrontation because we perceive it as danger. We yearn for the confrontation to be over, and this sometimes makes us compromise, and do or say the wrong thing.

Let's look at a few examples of this in the workplace.

> ➤ Have you ever put off a difficult phone call, never to actually make the call? I know I used to.
> ➤ Have you ever agreed with a difficult person, just to avoid confrontation?
> ➤ Have you ever given away information under pressure, you know you probably shouldn't have?
> ➤ Have you ever let a person get away with doing something you should have stopped them from doing, for fear of confrontation?

If you have aspirations of running a business, you must be able to confront difficult situations, with all types of people. If you are not able to do this, you must learn, or you'll struggle in business.

Let's assume you are at a networking event. You meet a competitor, who asks you to divulge some sensitive information. He promises not to tell anyone, but you politely refuse. He asks again, putting you under pressure. You refuse again. He promises you a favour in return if you tell him, and now you feel very pressured. You eventually give in and spill the beans. The pressure's off, the bad hormones go away and it feels good.

Then the worries start. Will he tell someone? Worse, will it get back to your boss? You begin to feel bad and you feel another sort of pressure brought on by your feeling of guilt.

So, what's going on in the body? Unconsciously we are associating the pressure with a threat. Our body reacts to a threat with hormones designed to help us fight or flight. Adrenaline and Cortisol flood the body and it doesn't feel good. You are under attack. You yearn for the feel-good hormones and it's these emotions which eventually lead to us compromising our integrity.

How many of us can truly say we haven't fallen victim to this kind of pressure? I certainly did in my younger day, but not for many years. Now I understand what is happening inside my body when I'm under this sort of pressure. I know that the hormone response will only last a couple of minutes, so I hang-in there and put off the need to feel good at the time, for doing the right thing, and feeling good later.

I can remember as a young surveyor, when I'd go to estimate a job. Often the client would ask how much it would be. I'd always have a figure in my head, but wouldn't disclose it. Once that figure was in their head, there was no changing it later. But still they'd apply the pressure – "come on, I won't tell anyone". I'd try not to give in, but a few times I did. "Ok, it's about £50,000" or whatever I thought it was.

Later, when I'd work out the quote accurately, and it came to £60,000, without exception, they'd say, "but you said £50".

I'd compromised myself, and there was no going back.

Never ever do it. Stand firm. If you compromise yourself, no one will trust you and you'll get a reputation. If you stand firm, they may not like it at the time, but they'll trust and want to work with you in the future.

One of the truest tests of integrity is its blunt refusal to be compromised. Your reputation is everything in business: protect it at all costs.

## DISHONESTY WILL HOLD YOU BACK

I'll leave you with one more story on integrity meant to prove how even the slightest lapses will hold you back in life.

A good friend of mine, Doug, had a solid business and was coming up to retirement. He had no family to hand the firm on to, but he did have two very good managers, Jake and Alan. He wanted to invite one of those to run his business and was struggling to choose between the two. It was difficult because they were both very good at what they did.

Jake, a very intelligent and talented manager, had been with the firm eight years, and had made a big impact. In his private life Jake was a party animal; he liked the booze and the ladies. This sometimes made him a little unreliable. It wasn't that he ever dropped the ball, but the potential was always there. For example, he'd turn up ten minutes late for a meeting, telling you the traffic was bad. He'd say he was going to pop into work on a Saturday to see how it was going, and not turn up. Little things, tiny untruths that niggled Doug. But Jake was talented and earned the firm money.

Alan was also a good manager but maybe not such a high achiever as Jake. He'd been with the company for seven years. Alan didn't take on as much work as Jake, but what he did do was always quality. Alan was the steadier of the two, a family man; if Alan said he was going to do something, he did it.

Let me ask you, who would you choose to take over your business and why?

Doug, a wise old dog, had been in business for years. He devised a plan to help him make the decision. He'd ask Jake and Alan to meet him at a random place, Southampton pier at 4am on Tuesday morning, giving no reason but that it was important that they were there.

This was at least a three-hour drive for both men, but after a little questioning, they both agreed to meet the boss at the dock.

Doug was there for 3.45am. When he arrived, Alan was already there and handed Doug a coffee. Jake called at 4.30, saying the traffic on the A3 was bad and he'd be there around 5am.

Now, who would you chose to run your business?

The moral to this story.

A solid, honest person will always get promoted over a talented person with poor values any day. Good values always win through in the end.

# SKILL 6

## WORRY - STRESS - ANXIETY

I am old enough to know for sure that stress, over a sustained period, is a killer. The problem is that we business owners are in the firing line for stress. To protect yourself you need to understand the subject, and in particular:

- ➢ When you are stressed.
- ➢ How bad the stress is.
- ➢ How to manage stress.

There have been times when I didn't think I could handle the pressure. I've had many sleepless nights and on occasions developed heart palpitations, which are very scary indeed. When you get to this stage, it's time to change something before it's too late.

The biggest worry I've had in business is lack of work and still having to pay the overheads. Overheads don't just disappear because you have no work; they leave your bank account regardless, month on month, regular as clockwork.

The second has been making mistakes. Most of our mistakes have been caused by poor attention to detail at pricing stage, where we estimated wrongly. This has cost us big sums of money. More than £250,000 on one occasion and several other large amounts over the years. This is quite stressful.

Fairly early on in my career, I came to the conclusion that I needed to learn about stress. I needed to be a master manager of stress, or I knew it would make me ill or even kill me at a young age, like it does so many others.

I read all I could on the subject including a great book called Overcoming Anxiety, by Helen Kennerley, which I'd strongly recommend you read.

Over the years I've developed a strategy for dealing with stress, which I hope will help you.

I see stress as three levels, each getting worse. Worry, leading to stress, leading to anxiety. Anxiety being the killer.

## MANAGING WORRY

I see worries as issues to deal with, that are under our control. You just need to take action quickly to stop worries from becoming stressful. Organisation techniques can really help here such as those in Skill 8. Use a to-do list, plan your time and most of all, take action quickly – stress is just around the corner.

If you have multiple tasks and are beginning to worry, here are some things you can do to help get back in the safe zone:

> ➤ Use the planning techniques in Skill 17.
> ➤ Use the organisational techniques in Skill 8.
> ➤ Act quickly, instantly if you can.

> ➤ Delegate some tasks as in Skill 10.
> ➤ Inform colleagues and ask for help.
> ➤ Work later in the short-term.
> ➤ Work weekends in the short-term.
> ➤ Give up hobbies in the short-term.

## MANAGING STRESS

Stress is usually brought on by long-term worry or fear over the thought of a future event. When you are stressed, hormones are released giving the fight or flight response. Sustained over a long period, this will damage your body, as vital immune functions are shut down when the body is stressed.

It may seem counter-productive, but if you are stressed, you must stop, and take time out to discover what is bothering you. Often the cause is obvious, a deal you are about to do that doesn't feel right, a project that's costing you money, or a partnership you are about to enter that doesn't feel right, even though on paper it looks good.

Your unconscious always knows what's right for you: trust it; it's evolved to work out what's good or bad for us over millions of years. Talking to loved ones and close friends can really help you make a decision too.

Then once you are sure what the problem is, make a decision and deal with it quickly. As soon as you do, it will feel better.

If the stress is down to short-term workload, maybe due to a busy period, use the techniques above for worry, put in more time in the short-term, maybe give up hobbies. I love to work-out most mornings – things have to be pretty tough before I'll give that up – but there have been times in my career, I've not worked out for months, because I've had to get a job done.

I'm not saying make this a way of life, I'm saying sometimes in business, you have to cut out things and prioritise.

## MANAGING ANXIETY

Sometime in your career, there is a very good chance that you will experience anxiety. I want you to be ready.

Anxiety can be long-term (chronic), or caused instantly, perhaps by news of a severe financial problem in your business, or worse, a problem with a loved one.

You'll know it's anxiety because there will be physical symptoms. Chronic anxiety can be a killer. Its cause is usually associated with a fear of an uncertain future, especially an uncertain financial future, or perhaps when we are pushing ourselves into bigger challenges, as we tend to in business.

I've experienced symptoms a few times in my career, when I was too busy over a sustained period, and when I was growing the business and taking on large debt, high risk or taking the business into new areas. You will experience no worse anxiety that the fear of going into old age with financial worries, but more about that later.

It's difficult to describe anxiety, but the best I can give you is that your mind is out of control, with our heart pumping fast, even at rest. No amount of meditation would calm me down. My mind wanted to sabotage my body.

As with worry and stress, try to be consciously aware that you are in an anxious state. Do not bury your head in the sand, get the problem out in the open, tell friends and family, colleagues and your employer. Get help and get serious about sorting this out. Use the techniques discussed above. Your health is most certainly being affected in some way.

Read-up on the subject, and be prepared.

One last thing on anxiety. Don't expect it to disappear overnight. In my experience, it can take weeks or months to reverse the symptoms. Just slowly use the techniques above, get lots of sleep, eat well and organise yourself. It will subside.

## THE NIGHT SWEATS

I wanted to talk to you specifically about this, as it will probably happen to you at some stage.

Have you ever woken up at night sweating? I can't tell you how many nights I've woken up in the middle of the night stressing about some issue at work. My dad used to say that's instinct telling you something isn't right. I've lived by that.

I have added this line in at 3.15am, as I'm stressing slightly about getting this book off to the publisher.

If I wake up worrying about the same thing a few times, I know something isn't right. I've learned to trust my instincts and there is considerable scientific evidence to support this.

In the book Sapiens: a brief history of humankind, Yuval Noah Harari discusses that humans have honed their instinct for danger over millions of years. They can 'feel' danger. A tiger behind a tree, someone about to attack, or maybe a bad deal you are about to make. Go against your instinct at your peril.

When I wake up with night sweats, I usually get up, go downstairs, and think about what's bothering me, like I am doing right now. The next day I do further due diligence, and I talk to trusted family, colleagues and mentors about my concerns. I've found in nearly all cases I trust my instincts, and don't do the deal.

## LIVING ON THE EDGE

I'm afraid, if you want wealth and freedom, you must be able to face your fears and deal with the pressures of stress.

Living on the edge of risk isn't a comfortable place to be, and a balance needs to be drawn between pushing yourself and facing new challenges, and ending up with anxiety. Keep yourself in balance. If the challenge is too big for you now, walk away, live to fight another day.

One thing is for sure, though. If you lack the temperament to deal with stress, please don't think of a career as an entrepreneur, because no amount of understanding or techniques will help you.

# SKILL 7

## ORGANISATIONAL SKILLS

I've found organisational skills are rarely taught in business; it's just one of those skills people assume they have, it's not really thought about, but it has such big implications to your life. If you find yourself running a business or managing people without organisational skills, you'll find yourself in a world of trouble and stress.

Organisation is one of those things that catches many people out in business, because they rarely give it the thought it deserves. They underestimate how important it is, especially as they take on more responsibility.

Many people keep things in their head, and then wonder why they wake up at night stressing over things they've forgotten. Then they can't get back to sleep in case they don't remember to do something in the morning.

Living like this is stressful. We discussed worry, stress and anxiety in the last section, so you have an understanding of the damage that anxiety can do to your body. So please take on the techniques we discuss here, and get your life under control. If you don't, you can forget about running a business for long, because you'll be forgetting to do things, letting people down and losing clients.

You need to get really good at this. As an entrepreneur or senior manager, you'll not only be planning your own time, but other people's too. It can get complicated. I'd like to share with you a technique that has worked for me for many years.

I've tried many systems to organize myself, but keep coming back to one my old secretary taught me. Let's take a look at a simple, but effective system called 'the bring forward system' of organisation.

## THE BRING FORWARD SYSTEM

I owe much of my organisational knowledge to my old secretary Joyce. She was an ex city personal assistant and a master organiser. She taught me about the bring forward system, and it will help you manage and prioritise your tasks, and never forget anything again.

The system works with the combination of a to-do list, and a calendar.

## PART 1. TO-DO LIST

During the day, you must get into the habit of writing everything down that will need your attention sometime in the future, on your to-do list, no matter how small the task. Jot them down in no particular order. The idea is to get the task out of your head.

I use Google notes to randomly list items on my mobile phone, because it syncs with my computer. But there are many to-do apps out there; the important thing is they must sync across devices.

Now you have accumulated your to-do list, the next thing is to plan when you want to do the task. This happens during your daily planning (see Skill 17).

## PART 2. CALENDAR

During daily planning time, review your to-do list.

You are asking yourself: When do I want or need to do this task, is there a deadline, is it urgent? Should I do it tomorrow, next week or month, or even now? Always choose now, if you can.

When you've decided when you want to do the task, remove it from your to-do list and put it into your diary, at a time you want to deal with it. Then forget about it until then.

For example, let's assume the accountant is coming on the 28th of each month to do management accounts. You need to have prepared work in progress for him (Skill 40), but you don't want to think about that until the 26th. But at the same time, you don't want to forget to do it. Plan it in for the 26th, allocate a time slot, and then rest easy until then.

The important thing is to plan every day, either first or last thing. Remove from the to-do list and on to your diary. This will keep your to-do list manageable and your diary planned well in advance.

The bring forward system keeps you organised, gives you peace of mind and keeps stress at bay.

## ORGANISING OTHERS

We discuss delegation in Skill 10, and as a business owner you'll have to organise your team's time, as you delegate tasks and projects. Without a system, this can become very confusing and stressful. There have been times when I've forgotten what I've delegated to whom.

The system I've developed is again simple. I've found if they are not simple, they don't work. I use Google notes and calendar as before.

First, set up a shared Google notes and calendar and add a colour code for each person.

Agree the project to be delegated or task to be done and plan it on the joint calendar.

Add in joint notes as you go along and meet regularly to review progress and allocate more tasks.

I've found it an effective way to keep remote contact with my team while keeping in the loop with their progress.

## BUSINESS AND PERSONAL ORGANISING

When people ask me where I work, I say I have no work, I just have my life. My life is work and my work is my life. Organisation for me is simple: I run a joint to-do list for my work and my personal life. I do colour code, though, for personal social events with my partner, or business events. My partner and I have a joint calendar so she can add events into our joint diary.

## MORNING ROUTINE

There's a great book called the Miracle Morning by Hal Elrod, which talks about the benefits of getting up early to carry out a routine. Many other personal development speakers, such as Robin Sharma, speak about the 5am club, and the benefits of an early morning routine, which includes exercise, meditation, affirmations, motivational videos and planning.

At various times in my life I've tried the 5am club, and I must admit I found it amazing, a massive head-start on the day, but unsustainable for me. I much prefer to stay up a little later, say 10-10.30 planning the next day and reviewing my goals. I never watch television apart from the odd Friday evening, then rise around 7.30am; this suits my body clock. Whatever works for you is fine. The important thing is to plan religiously at least every work night or morning.

I call my evening routine, generically, planning time, and the whole family knows what I am doing. In fact, this is what I'm actually doing.

- ➢ I'm taking items off my to-do list, bringing them forward into my diary and allocating them a time slot.
- ➢ I'm reviewing and amending my plans toward my goals.
- ➢ I'm revisiting my goals, creating repetition to get them deep in my mind.
- ➢ I also deal with emails all in one go.

I finish the one to two-hour session with a clear head, so I can go to bed and feel totally on top of things and get a good night's sleep.

# SKILL 8

## MOTIVATION

An old manager of mine, Bill, and I were discussing ways of motivating the labourers one day, when he said...

"The problem is, Ray, I have to motivate people to dig holes in the mud, in the rain, day after day and be happy about it. How do I do that?"

How would you do it? The answer is very complicated, as we shall see. Motivation is unique to all of us – what works for one person will definitely not work for another.

I didn't tell Bill at the time that I was once that labourer digging trenches in the rain. I was trying to remember what motivated me. I think maybe the money, praise from the boss, praise from my dad, fear of getting sacked, determination and a will to develop myself, so I wouldn't ever have to dig trenches again.

Like many subjects of the mind I find this one fascinating, and you should too if you want to manage people.

I've employed hundreds of people over the years, and I've tried almost as many ways to motivate them. I got it wrong a lot in the early days, but as my experience and education grew, my results improved, and I feel qualified to give you good advice on the subject.

The problem with motivation is that most of us don't even know what motivates us. Many motivators come from deep within our unconscious mind, like my early need for achievement, driven by a constant search of my dad's approval.

But some are more obvious, such as the arrival of a new baby and the need for a bigger house with another bedroom.

There are differing schools of thought on motivation, and it's good to understand the theory.

## FREUD

According to Sigmund Freud, most human behaviour is the result of desires, impulses and memories that have been repressed into the unconscious mind, yet still influence actions. These unconscious motivators are the 'real' reasons we do things.

An example could be when someone is driven by achievement, as I was. Such a person could have no understanding of why they are so driven, and that situation could carry on for a lifetime. But occasionally, through personal development or counselling, one can become self-aware, and realise in an instant that the need to achieve came from lack of parental attention or praise, setting off the never-ending quest to seek approval.

On a side note. I confronted my father about this one day, and he said, "Well it got you where you are today, didn't it?" I couldn't argue with that.

## MASLOW

Abraham Maslow came at this from a different angle. His famous Hierarchy of Needs explains that people must first fulfil one level of human needs before they can move on to a higher level. As shown below.

I can remember when we were expecting our first son. I didn't feel particularly financially secure, and that focussed my mind. Other less important activities such as hobbies and going out with friends took a back seat, and I worked all the hours until I felt secure again. At which point we began more of a social life.

Understanding Freud and Maslow is a great help to you as a business owner or manager in understanding staff. If you study the hierarchy, you will understand where others are on the hierarchy, and how best to help or motivate these individuals towards the next level.

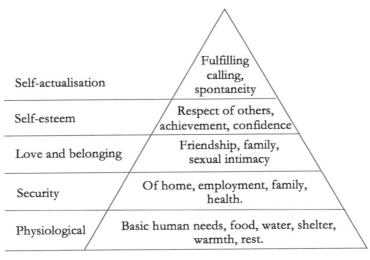

Abraham Maslow's hierarchy of Needs

## MOTIVATORS

Finding the best way to motivate a person is difficult, make that very difficult. People have rarely come into my office and said, "I would really value a new car because keeping up with the neighbours is very important to me". Or, "I'm having an affair and need more money to spend on the other woman". Although we do have one guy at the moment who will tell you he wants the best car in his street.

He is easy to motivate, but with most people you'll need to work a little harder. I've found the best way to understand how to motivate individuals is to give them your time, ask them for a coffee, find out what's going on in their lives. Get to know and understand what is important to them. Then, a picture will emerge, you'll begin to understand the person, and their needs at this time in their life.

I've listed some of the things that I have found are important to people over the years:

- ➢ Money
- ➢ Autonomy
- ➢ Development
- ➢ Power
- ➢ Status
- ➢ Title
- ➢ Flexibility
- ➢ Pat on the back
- ➢ Giving your time
- ➢ Being treated with respect

## DE-MOTIVATORS

I've found without fail, the reasons people leave a company have to do with other people. Of-course, people leave over money on occasions, but then it is usually reluctantly.

One survey I read said that being unnoticed is the worst form of anxiety at work. People would rather the boss shouted at them than not notice them.

This is the top list I could find of things that de-motivate staff:

> ➤ Uncaring boss
> ➤ Negative colleagues
> ➤ Being ignored (the biggie)
> ➤ Low wage
> ➤ Not receiving recognition
> ➤ No progression route (especially for non-family members in family businesses)

## ONE SIZE 'DOESN'T' FIT ALL

You can never generalise with motivation, we are all so very different. If ever there was a time when the term 'one size fits all' wasn't relevant, it's here. Look at some of the variables:

> ➤ Our upbringings
> ➤ Our life experiences
> ➤ Our expectations
> ➤ What's going on in our lives
> ➤ What stage of life we are at

You can begin to understand that motivation is an individual situation, not a group situation; that's why many incentive schemes fail. I know, I've tried most.

The best way I've found to motivate my team is to treat them as individuals, try to understand what is happening in their lives and do my best to help them however I can. I've never had a person leave since I learned that.

## MOTIVATION CAN CHANGE VERY QUICKLY OR OVER TIME

Motivation is a moving target; it can change very quickly. Just when you think you have found the formula that motivates a person, something in their life changes. I'll give you an example of something that happened to us.

A site manager I'd considered very content worked for us for years. He didn't seem to be motivated by money, but a kind word and a pat on the back now and then went down well. He didn't like doing overtime, and rarely asked for a pay rise. I had him down as a happy and contented plodder.

One day my project manager told me he was leaving. I was surprised and asked him to my office to find out why.

He said his wife had fallen pregnant with their first baby a week ago, and that he needed to earn more money. I offered him more, and he stayed with us.

Without us knowing, overnight his priorities had changed. His motivation was now completely different from the previous day: now it was money, not job satisfaction.

There are many examples of how someone's motivation can change quickly or slowly, but here's just a few:

> Someone who has just taken on a big mortgage.
> A separation or divorce can lead to the person needing time off and more support.
> Illness in family or personally could mean more time off or flexible working becomes important.

In my experience, people often do not bring these issues to your attention, so you're left wondering why they are acting differently or why they have left.

The lesson here, again, is to keep close to your main people, and send this message down the line to your managers to do the same. Invite them for a coffee now and then, find out what's going on in their lives. Ask how you can help. If you do this, you'll have a motivated, happy and loyal team.

One more tip for you, on keeping in the loop with your team: the management 'mole'. I used to have a van driver years ago. He was a notorious gossip. I invited him in for a coffee now and then, to find out what was really going on with the team. He seemed to enjoy it, and I learned the inside gossip. He's a cab driver now!

## FINANCIAL INCENTIVES

I've tried many incentive schemes over the years, and in my experience, not many work. The only time they may do is when the person is paid on commission, say in sales.

But this is rarely the case with managers and the senior team, also most office 9-5 staff. In fact, in my experience, not only do financial incentives not work, they can cause problems. It can create rivalry between team members, who sometimes perceive their talents to be more than their peers, yet the reward scheme favours all equally.

The other main problem with financial incentives is that when management come-up with these schemes, it's generally at a time when the business is doing well. But a trough always follows a peak in business. Giving away 1% percent of net profits seemed like a good idea then, but now it's suicide, and management have to squirm out of the deal.

In my experience, there is only one way to motivate people. You have to know your team, as well as you can. I'm not talking superficially, I'm talking their upbringing, family life, hobbies, and work history; leave no stone unturned. The more you know the better you'll be able to help them and help your business. A win-win situation.

## AUTONOMY

Another good way I've found to keep a person happy and content, is to give them as much freedom and autonomy as your business will allow, and do as much as you can to facilitate the changing circumstances in their life.

When I employ a person, I say something like, "You can manage your own time, work the hours you need to work. You are free to go the dentist, get your hair done or whatever you need to do. I get these benefits, and so will you. The only thing I ask in return, is that you are honest with me, as I will be with you."

I've found with this policy, few people, if any, ever leave my companies. Why would they? I'm offering them autonomy, and that sits well with most humans.

One note of caution.

Some people just don't get the freedom policy. They have the wrong values, maybe they are too far gone down the 9-5 control model, who knows? But some people take advantage of the system. They are unable to be honest, and if so, we let them go.

The other strange thing I've noticed, is that even though the team are aware of the policy, they rarely use it. They sit there 9-5 and still ask if it's ok to go to the dentist. It's amazing. Old habits die hard, I suppose.

# SKILL 9

## THE ART OF DELEGATION

I learned very early on in business, that if I didn't want to carry on doing everything myself, I'd have to get good at delegation.

I'd go so far as to say, if you can't master this skill, you'll be doomed to the operational ranks, doing it yourself forever, like so many other people. But there's more to delegation than just offloading work, so read on.

I always think delegation is an art, because it involves having a very good understanding of human nature.

### WHAT IS DELEGATION?

The Google definition is: "The action or process of delegating or being delegated".

That's not very helpful, so let's take a deeper look.

## WHO CAN YOU DELEGATE TO?

> ➤ You can ask a junior – delegating down.
> ➤ Your boss can ask you – delegating down.
> ➤ You can also ask your boss – delegating up (if you're brave enough).
> ➤ You can ask a colleague – delegating sideways.
> ➤ You can delegate to anyone – everyone is a resource to an entrepreneur.

When I have something to do I scan my entire network of people, both in and outside work, including acquaintances and friends of friends. Be really resourceful.

## WHY DELEGATE

When I ask my mentees why they must delegate, the normal reply is, to get more done, or because I'm busy. These are true, and there are a few more important reasons I've learned over the years that you must know to run a business.

## TOO MUCH TO DO

Perhaps you do have too many tasks to deal with. Perhaps you are feeling stressed with the workload or at risk of dropping the ball, or worse, letting someone down or compromising on quality. It's time to ask for help and delegate some of the work.

## DEVELOPMENT OF JUNIORS

Delegation is essential in developing juniors. I've found many managers miss this. You don't just delegate to a junior to ease your workload, a good manager looks for opportunities to delegate specific tasks she feels the junior would benefit from. Asking a junior to carry out a task just on the edge of their comfort zone will keep them interested and motivated. Soon you'll have a competent person, and this in turn will allow you to move up. As I've said to my managers, if you want to move up, find someone who can do your job as well as or better than you

A note of caution here. I've had a few managers who are reluctant to delegate to juniors, especially talented ones, because they are frightened the person will overtake them, and take their job.

Be on the watch out for this. If you catch it happening, talk to the offending manager and reassure them in the first instance. If the problem persists, part company and promote the junior. There is nothing worse than an insecure manager holding back talent. There are deep rooted reasons why people do this, but you are not a counsellor, you are responsible for the team.

A good manager not only thinks of the junior, but delegates to leverage her own time for the more important duties. It's a win-win.

## TO FREE TIME UP FOR PLANNING

Part of your role as senior manager is strategy. Improvements today for the good of tomorrow. Planning time is essential for managers; I recommend 80% of the time doing, 20% planning to do (see Skill 20).

The more you master the art of delegation, the less you'll be bogged down in day-to-day tasks, and the more time you'll have for strategic planning. The more you plan, the higher you will go in the organisation. Your ultimate aim is to delegate yourself out of operations altogether.

## WHAT CAN BE DELEGATED

The simple answer is, anything. It matters not what you delegate, what matters is that you find the right person to delegate to. This is where your skill must lie.

You could delegate simple or complex tasks. I delegate all of my personal administration and the running of three entire businesses. Richard Branson has over four hundred businesses according to Google.

My formula is to find the right person and work out what motivates them. Give them autonomy and responsibility. Provide ongoing support and encouragement. Set up reporting systems and meet regularly.

I've set up formal reporting for my main business. I meet one day per month with my son Ben, the MD of our construction business, to run through the financials and future strategy. He leaves the meeting feeling supported and I leave feeling reassured. We also use the meeting as a mentoring vehicle, slowly but surely transferring knowledge from one generation to the next. It works well.

I never interfere with the way he runs the business, but I'm always there to offer my experience, which he needs less and less these days.

## TO DEVELOP YOURSELF

As you develop others through delegation, so you develop yourself in carrying out higher level tasks and managing people. If you do not delegate, but continue to do tasks yourself, you are stifling your development. Life moves on; you, in effect, go backwards.

The entrepreneur's mind-set when asked to do something is, think not how can I do it, think, who can I get to do it?

## OWNING THE RESPONSIBILITY

One of my main issues with managers and delegation, is that so few understand this simple but very important concept, of owning the responsibility.

The person who delegates the task retains responsibility, unless otherwise agreed. Very important and so often the cause of mistakes. I'm going to say that again so it sinks in.

The person who delegates the task, retains responsibility, unless otherwise agreed.

If a bricklayer falls to his death on a building site, the chief executive goes to prison. That's how responsibility works. You do not delegate the responsibility, only the task. I've found many managers delegate the task, then hope for the best. That's brushing it under the carpet, and it never works; it just comes back to you to sort out the mess, and takes even more of your time.

If you delegate a report to your assistant, to be on the boss's desk by Friday, you need to monitor her progress and the quality of

65

the report. If the report is shoddy or isn't ready, guess who gets the chop? It's no good blaming the junior – the boss asked you, you are responsible.

So many mistakes happen like this. The junior forgetting to do something, or doing it wrong. But the manager took no interest in the junior's progress. Then blames the junior when it goes wrong.

In the same way, if our building firm were to go under, I'd not blame my son, it'd be down to me. I delegated the running of the firm to him. That's why I've set-up monthly financial reporting so I can keep a watchful eye on things. If I suspect something is not right, I delve in deeper. My passive income depends on me protecting my investment. It's a question of responsibility.

## THE DELEGATION MIND-SET

Most of the managers I've worked with delegate to some degree. Some are good at it and get promoted quickly. But then invariably, boom, they hit the delegation glass ceiling.

I'd like a pound for every time I've heard a really good manager say,

"I delegate most things, but I keep this for myself, because it's so important".

For many years this was me. That's why I was stuck in the business, there was no one else who could do this particular thing as well as me. Haha it makes me laugh now...of course, I'm the only person in the world who can do it this well.

In NLP, they call this a limiting belief. It limited me to work in the company for years. But eventually I learned to find talent, train talent, move on and check in occasionally, and my life changed.

So please, never fall into my trap. There is always someone better than you for the job. You may be an amazing accountant, but trust me, there's a better one out there. Anyway, you are not being paid to be an accountant, you are running the show. Find someone better than you, and move on.

To recap, the entrepreneur mind-set when presented with a task is:

### Who can I get to do this?

The secret to progress through the ranks of any company, or to run multiple companies is to:

- ➤ Find the right talent.
- ➤ Train the talent.
- ➤ Offer support when required.
- ➤ Monitor progress.

Don't tell the boss I told you, but this alone is a big part of the secret to progression, within any company.

## WHO YOU CAN'T DELEGATE TO

So far, we have spoken about those we can delegate to. But there are many people that you can't, or shouldn't, delegate to. Many people get caught out by this, and it is your job to identify these people before they do damage.

I had a site manager many years ago, Big Bob, a very talented carpenter, good with the guys, so I asked him to manage some sites. Big Bob must have called me six times a day, asking what he should do about this and that. Small things like, should he call the client, or where should he position site signs and so on. It became unbearable.

I asked him to my office for a chat to find out why he called so often. He said, "I don't want to take the responsibility if something goes wrong." Surprised, I pursued it further. He was unable to sleep at night "with that kind of pressure".

Pressure? I was truly shocked. His threshold for responsibility was so low I couldn't believe it. Some people take responsibility for an entire country; this guy couldn't take responsibility for where the signs go.

Through my time in business, I've learned that size or gender is irrelevant: some people cannot deal with responsibility – actually, most people in my experience.

So, before you delegate, make sure the person can handle it. You may not know at first, so monitor more in the early days. If they seem comfortable with what you are asking them to do, release a little more responsibility. Never assume they are as resilient as you.

Generally speaking, entrepreneurs have a high threshold for responsibility, both taking it and giving it. If yours is low, work on it. Or you'll never run businesses.

## BEWARE DELEGATING TO THE PERSON THAT ALWAYS SAYS YES

This is another personality type not to delegate to. I've been caught out more than once by people saying yes to everything. I'm sure there are deep psychological reasons for not being able to say no. The need to please, or the fear of confrontation is too strong in some people.

First of all, they appear amazing. When the boss asks, "who can take this project on", they are the first to volunteer, often overloading themselves with work. Then the inevitable happens: it all goes wrong.

When you ask why things went wrong, they say, "I was too busy", or, "I forgot". Well, why the hell did you take it in the first place?!

I've found some common traits in these people. They often smile a lot, and agree with everything you say. Their need to please often outweighs their ability to say no.

The irony is, this personality type generally rises through the ranks quickly, because they are amenable and easy to manage. But long-term, they can do damage, especially if they are in a position to negotiate on behalf of your business.

Find them out, and let them go.

I'd rather deal with a person that says it how it is, any day. It may not be comfortable to hear your manager say no at the time. But believe me, long term you learn to trust that person and give them more responsibility.

# SKILL 10

## RELATIONSHIPS

By now you're probably realising the importance I put on relationships, and I hope you will learn to, too. Here I take a deeper look at some specific relationships and how they can affect your business and life. You may be surprised at the ones I consider most important.

### RELATIONSHIPS AND HAPPINESS

For over 75 years, the Harvard's Grant and Glueck study has tracked the physical and emotional well-being of 724 men.

They've diligently analysed blood samples, conducted brain scans and pored over self-reported surveys, to compile the findings.

The conclusion was that one thing surpasses all the rest in terms of happiness.

"The clearest message that we get from this 75-year study is this: Good relationships keep us happier and healthier. Period."

The biggest predictor of your happiness and fulfilment overall in life, is basically love.

## THE BIGGEST DECISION YOU'LL EVER MAKE

The choice of life partner is, in my experience, by far the biggest decision you'll ever make. Simply because it can either be the source of the most amazing support, enabling you to be free to build your empire. Or, if it goes wrong, have the most devastating effect on your emotional state, business, finances and of course, children.

They say that buying a house is the biggest decision most people make, but believe me, that pales into insignificance beside your choice of life partner.

I was married at the age of twenty-four. I met and married within six months. Like all my friends and many young people, I didn't think it through, it just felt natural. I was ready for commitment, so we married. Big mistake.

Let me ask you a question. If you were in business, and someone offered you a large contract you knew had a fifty percent chance of going wrong, and would cost you over half your business if it did, would you do it? Who in their right mind would put themselves in that position? I did when I married the wrong person, and many other business owners I know tell me similar stories.

I was lucky: I didn't lose half my business, but I lost every personal asset I had, a large unencumbered home, pensions, cash and a lot of goods I'd built up over the years.

Not just that, the emotional turmoil is staggering. If there was ever anything that could decimate a business, it's the turmoil of a divorce. Especially where children are involved.

So, can you begin to understand that your choice of partner in life is by far the biggest decision you'll ever make, and should be treated as such?

My partner said I was wasting my time putting this section in the book, as where love is concerned, people don't listen to logic. But I have a responsibility to you in this book, to bring this to your attention. Please think deeply about your partner in life as you would any other big commitment. This means taking your time to get to know the person – at least two years, in my experience, maybe more.

I feel it's even more important for a business owner, as generally speaking, they will have built up assets, and in law your entire estate is at risk in a divorce.

## BEHIND EVERY GREAT MAN

It is fairly undisputed that behind every great man, there is a great woman, and vice versa. The evidence for this is overwhelming. This makes it even more important to choose the right partner. The benefits of having a supportive partner are many.

I am perhaps a good example. When I became managing director aged twenty-eight, the company progressed every year. I had support at home and could really focus on the business. My children were looked after by my wife at home and the house was taken care of, leaving me free to push-on with the business and provide a great life for us all.

Then the divorce at thirty-nine. The following year, turnover halved. My head was all over the place, my focus was on our children, who came to live with me and the business had to take second place.

It was years before I could really focus on the business again. A single parent bringing up four young sons and a struggling business. I'd be driving to a business meeting, when all I could think about was we had no fruit at home. I had to be available for school activities and collections at short notice when they were sick. I certainly have empathy for single working parents.

It carried on like this until around ten years later, when I met my new lady. But it took a long four years of getting to know her before I committed this time. I wasn't going to make the same mistake again. But eventually we settled together, and as if by magic, my business followed. Turnover shot-up, and I started new businesses. I had support at home and was free to focus again. She provided me the support and purpose I needed to provide us both with a great lifestyle.

These are the benefits I get from our relationship. She:

> Listens to me talk about my ideas and gives me feedback.
> Helps me see things from other perspectives.
> Gives me encouragement.
> Gives me her opinion on risks I'm about to take. Which is usually, go for it.
> Gives me unwavering support.
> Looks after our home so my mind can be free to focus.
> Provides intimacy and emotional support.

> ➤ Is a partner in life.
> ➤ Enables me to be all I can be.
> ➤ Gives me a 'purpose' to build something meaningful.

Taking emotions out of the equation, the fact is, that for most of us, our primary relationship underpins all we do. This is why this section found its way into my book.

I hope this has made you understand how significant the choice of life partner is. So be nice to your partner, don't take him or her for granted and understand what they enable you to achieve in your life. When you realise this, you will certainly prioritise this relationship.

## RELATIONSHIPS WITH EMPLOYEES

In my experience, it's near impossible to be friends with your employees. Sometimes it's lonely at the top, and it's tempting to make confidants of employees. But please resist this temptation.

I didn't always think like this. I used to try to make friends of some of my managers, and meet outside of work, sometimes with their families. But the problem is, that businesses sometimes go through difficult times, and you may have to let a friend go. Then you've lost a friend, and you feel bad. It's then you realise, you can't make friends with staff.

It works the other way round too. I had a manager who shall remain nameless, but I'll call him Dick. Dick came to work for me as junior manager. I noticed his talent, so I encouraged his development and taught him a lot of what I know. He was with me for over ten years. In that time, we became great friends, or so I thought. Lunch and conversation most days, we knew each other very well.

One day out-of-the-blue, he asked for three months off, to "sort his head out", as he put it. He asked us to pay him for the time up-front, £24,000. I was put out, but I trusted him, so agreed.

We received a phone call two-weeks into his leave from a long-term client asking for Dick's company. We replied he was on leave, but she insisted he was carrying out work for her through his own business.

When we looked into the matter, we found out he'd set up his own business some months before in his wife's name, and was working for our clients, whilst still working for us. Had he told me of his intentions to start a business, I would have helped him set it up, and we could have remained friends, but he didn't have the integrity, and decided to do it the deceitful way, as employees often do in my experience.

The whole situation makes me smile now, but I was hurt at the time. Then I learned a valuable lesson: never get too close to your employees – their interests are different from yours. Be friendly, but not friends, and protect your assets at all costs.

The other thing I learned is not to let your employees get too close to your clients.

## RELATIONSHIPS WITH CLIENTS

Similar to that of staff, you cannot get too close. Get close enough to build a good working relationship, become good business associates, but their business interests and yours will inevitably go in different directions one day.

## RELATIONSHIPS WITH SUPPLIERS AND SERVICE PROVIDERS

An old mentor told me: "drive down prices of commodities, but pay over for a service". It's good advice.

There's no room to build relationships when buying commodities. You can buy, for example, timber, anywhere, so you may as well drive down the price.

On the other hand, pay well for a service. People providing a service to you, such as advisors, need to feel well remunerated to do their best work. It's here you pay the money and build the relationships.

# SKILL 11

## MISTAKES

Before I started in business, like most people, I didn't give mistakes much thought. However, once I was in business, the word took on a whole new meaning. Mistakes cost me money, sometimes a lot.

We are going to look into the various facets of mistakes, and I am going to pass on my experiences of dealing with mistakes in business, how they can be both useful and sometimes devastating.

I'm always nagging my sons about mistakes in their business. To me, they don't give mistakes the consideration they deserve. They talk to me about growing turnover, but rarely about mitigating mistakes. I tell them there are few things in business that can put you under more quickly than a big mistake. So, my advice is put as much energy into mitigating mistakes as you do about growing turnover. This means building checks in your systems.

The areas I've discussed below are partly from my psychological training, but mostly from my experience of employing and managing hundreds of people over the years.

## SMALL MISTAKES AND BIG MISTAKES

There are, as I call them, small and big mistakes. The small ones are good, as they can be opportunities, but the big ones are not good, and must be avoided at all costs.

To illustrate my point, here's what happened to a company called Excite.

In 1999 Google was a relatively new search engine, Excite at the time was number two. Larry Page offered to sell Google to Excite for under $1m, but was refused. I wonder how Excite feel about that decision now.

I've gone into more detail on how big mistakes can put you under in Skill 47, so I'll leave that here until then.

## MISTAKES AND SELF-CONFIDENCE

If someone were to tell me I've made a mistake, I'm one of those people who'd own up immediately, or more usually bring it to the attention of the team by announcing it loudly. That's because I'm confident in my abilities; I don't need to hide anything.

Some people, I've learned, are not like this. I worked with a manager who was so incapable of admitting a mistake, he would get aggressive and defensive, immediately blaming anyone or anything but himself.

Later, as I became more aware of human nature, I realised that owning up to mistakes has a lot to do with self-confidence, and that has a lot to do with upbringing and life experiences.

This is where getting to know your team is important. When I learned about his life, I wasn't surprised he was incapable of owning up. He was brought up in care homes with no positive role model. He'd spent the greater part of his childhood covering up and keeping below the radar. He had low self-esteem, low confidence, and was sure he'd be sacked if he made a mistake. His behaviour was so deep, whatever reassurance I gave him was futile.

I've found these people impossible to deal with – they cover things up, build covert alliances to cover their tracks, and you never get the truth out of them. They are dangerous and can damage relationships with your clients and cause discontent in your organisation.

Don't make the same mistake I did. Identify them quickly, and let them go.

## DEAL WITH A MISTAKE CALMLY

I've never forgotten my old boss Sid Swain. At age eighteen, he taught me the best way to deal with an employee who made a mistake.

As an apprentice toolmaker, I'd been working on a project for two weeks, I drilled a hole in the wrong place, and it virtually ruined the entire job. I went to the loo and sat for a while contemplating my next move. Then I went to face the boss.

I knocked on Sid's door expecting the worst. I told him what I'd done and to my surprise he didn't shout; he said calmly, "Ah, I see, laddie, let me come out with you, and we can find the best way forward". Not a raised voice or bad word. He spent a couple of hours with me and we worked out the best thing to do.

I respected him so much for that. When I became the boss, I realised how difficult that must have been for him to control his emotions and set me a good example.

Sid taught me not to fear making mistakes, but to learn from them. As the boss, I try never to chastise my team. Easier said than done, and I've not always been successful.

## DON'T MAKE THE SAME MISTAKE TOO MANY TIMES

On another occasion at Sid's firm, the outcome was very different. The firm took on apprentices every year. One lad became my friend. He wasn't particularly skilled and I covered for him a lot. One day he was summoned to Sid's office and came out crying. He'd been sacked.

This riled me, and I stormed into Sid's office to ask why. He said the lad was scared of machinery, and that sooner or later he'd hurt himself. This was why he made so many mistakes. He held up his hand to show me a finger with the tip cut off – he'd done it as a boy on a guillotine – to ram home the point, I think. It worked. He thought that the lad would be better off in a job that suited him.

As Sid's words came out I knew inside he was right. Moreover, I thought it was fair – the best thing for my friend in the long run was to find a job that he was suited to. Although he didn't think so at the time.

I learned two things from that. If the mistake is repeated following appropriate training, then the person is not right for the job. You have to let them go. It's cruel to be kind.

## MISTAKES ARE OPPORTUNITIES

In my younger day, I dreaded mistakes. Mistakes cost time and money, and I wasn't very nice to be around if someone had made a big bloomer

Then, over the years, I got wise and began to see the opportunity. In my NLP training, they called this reframing. I reframed the mistake to see where we could find the opportunity. I even began to welcome mistakes, dare I say, encourage mistakes. Sounds mad, right? – my staff thought so too – but I saw these mistakes as low hanging marketing fruit.

When a client called my company about a mistake they thought we had made (sometimes we hadn't even made the mistake), we politely agreed to return to site the same day to attend the issue. We followed up the visit with a phone call to ask if everything was satisfactory. My goal was to exceed their expectations, so they could have nothing but good to say about us and want to use us again.

We turned the mistake into a marketing opportunity no amount of money could buy, and it cost a few pounds to send a plumber round for an hour.

## FEELING BAD AFTER MAKING A MISTAKE

My sixteen-year-old son Alex asked me to put this section in. He said he felt bad after making a mistake, and wanted to understand more about that feeling.

He said he feels bad for some time after making a mistake. I told him that's natural, no one likes to make mistakes. But it's funny how we always focus on our few mistakes and not on our many victories. A good boss reminds his team of that. I told my son to recognise his many accomplishments and don't be so hard on himself. He'd only been working for ten months at the time, and was already managing all the purchase paperwork for fourteen properties.

When you've made a mistake and you are feeling bad, the trick is to understand that you've just had an opportunity to grow. Mistakes are just a natural part of personal growth, so as long as they are not big mistakes, don't worry, learn from them. Realise that on the edge of mistakes is where learning and personal development happens.

I've also realised that people who make a lot of mistakes do a lot of things. If you do a lot of things, it follows you will make a lot of mistakes. Entrepreneurs typically involve themselves in many things at once, so mistakes are bound to happen. So be proud of your mistakes.

As a boss, you should understand that your team will make mistakes; in a way, you want them to. It means they are learning and growing. Just keep checking they are learning from the experience, and not repeating the mistake, because if they are, you know what you have to do, I'm afraid.

## BRUSHING IT UNDER THE CARPET

Fred, we shall call him, our estimator at the time, won a large contract to refurbish a leisure centre. We later found an error of more than £70,000. We confronted Fred, who eventually admitted that he had guessed the price.

We contacted the client to ask if we could increase our price. There was nothing they could do, contracts had been drawn up. But, they added, since we'd been £100,000 cheaper, we could have increased our price, had we told them earlier.

I mentioned earlier that you shouldn't shout at an employee who makes a mistake. I have to confess that I did on this occasion, just before sacking him. Hiding that mistake cost the company £70,000 and that was inexcusable in my book. It was dishonest, and there only one thing to do with dishonest employees.

If you catch a team member hiding mistakes, you know what has to be done. It's tough love, I'm afraid. You are responsible to the team and you must protect their interests and your own.


## WHOSE FAULT IS IT REALLY

Remember this: no one makes a genuine mistake on purpose, ever. Unless they are trying to do you harm, but that's different.

I've found the reason is usually closer to home than you may want to hear. It's usually down to you, the boss, in one way or another.

- ➢ Inadequate systems and processes
- ➢ Over work
- ➢ Inadequate training

- ➢ Too much responsibility
- ➢ Wrong person for the job
- ➢ Not enough experience

All the above are the boss's responsibility, so before you explode, think about the real cause.

It matters little who made the mistake, much more important is to identify exactly how it happened. Then amend the process to ensure it can't happen again. Take the emotion out of it, focus on the wellbeing of the business. Broker a culture where owning up is encouraged, with no repercussions.

# SKILL 12

## AUTHENTICITY

If authenticity is "being who you are", then it follows that first, you must know who you are.

### KNOWING YOURSELF

So, this begs the question, do you know who you are? Have you ever really considered where you stand on various values, or compared your values with other people's? This is important, because your personal values will transfer directly into your business, so do some soul searching to know yourself before you get started in business.

Where do you stand on trust, loyalty, integrity, openness, commitment and all the other values? What's important to you and what's not? Some of us are lucky enough to have parents who instil good values in us at an early age. Some of us do not have that benefit, and have to learn from people we come across throughout the course of our life, who may or may not be good role models.

Therefore, one could be authentic to one's values, but the values themselves could be questionable. In this case you should search out people you respect with good values, and learn from them.

The matter is further complicated because we are all works in progress, so what our values are today may change tomorrow.

## TRADITIONAL VALUES

During my NLP training, I learned people skills techniques aimed at building rapport quickly.

These included body language techniques such as mirroring and matching the other person's body movements. Also, conversational techniques where we show an inordinate amount of interest in the other person, asking questions designed to make them talk about themselves. Then listening intently.

These are designed to make people feel comfortable with you, and like you. These techniques are very useful in interview situations, or where pitching your service to a new client.

However, many years after the training I read a book that changed my opinion regarding short-term persuasion.

It was a book on traditional values, and the book argued this:

> You can use all the modern-day, short-term, like-me-quick techniques you like, and they will work. They may get you the job or the girlfriend. But in time, when the honeymoon period is over, and your guard is down, your true values are bound to show through.

I never ever try to make someone like me now. I stay true to my values, and in time, if my values are similar to the other person's, we build a solid relationship. There is really no other way to keep a valued client over a long period. In fact, no other way to maintain any relationship.

## KEEP IT REAL

"When you show up authentic, you create the space for others to do the same."

**Anonymous**

"Think of a person you respect for his or her honesty, for his or her openness, for his or her integrity. This person feels real to you. Genuine. Authentic. It's refreshing to be around this person, to get to know this person, to interact with him or her."

**By Joshua Fields Millburn & Ryan Nicodemus**

Admittedly, like in the film Liar Liar where Jim Carrey was brutally honest, and hurt a few feelings in the process, there are a few occasions where it is difficult to be totally authentic. But leaders have to be authentic. This means knowing yourself and your values, and standing by those values. Having the courage to stand strong when someone is trying to compromise your values, as in Skill 5, integrity and trust.

Sometimes in the workplace, this means confronting situations, giving tough love rather than burying your head in the sand. Even if it means affecting the relationship with a colleague, or indeed your children, you must stand by your values.

## SMALL EXCEPTION TO THE RULE

In my business career, I've prided myself on being open; what's in my head comes out of my mouth, giving tough love on occasions, which I'm sure hasn't always made me popular.

But there have been a few times when I haven't been totally authentic. For example, I've been in interviews having been short-listed for a big project, and occasionally I've thought the client is talking absolute rubbish. As authentic as I like to think I am, I haven't the balls to tell the client what I'm thinking, because if I did, we'd surely lose the project, and I'd have let my team down.

When it comes to putting food on the table, I'll control my emotions and keep what's inside, inside. Within reason. But that's your call.

# SKILL 13

## CONFORMING

I was lucky enough to be apprenticed twice, the second time to a very skilled tradesman, Bert Johnson, who worked for my dad. A sixty-year-old, very traditional craftsman who had been in the building industry all his life. I was fresh out of my engineering career, this was my second career, and I was starting at the bottom again.

Bert was a lovely, caring man, who followed tradition to the letter. In the five years I was with him, he passed on his skills to me, and although no use to me now, to this day I can do just about anything the building trade requires. Much to my annoyance, as I still don't like anyone else working on my own home.

Although we became great friends, after a few months working together, the differences in our view of life began to show. One time he asked me to make a new drawer, for a cabinet. The drawer had what are known as dovetail joints in the corners, and we were remaking it because the joints had split.

I remade the drawer but altered the design of the dovetails to make them more robust. When Bert returned, he asked why I'd altered the design. I said because it had "cracked previously, and

I didn't want the same to happen again". He scolded me, saying, "Dovetails have always been made that way." I replied, "Just because they've always been made like that, doesn't mean they always have to." He was bemused; he didn't get it.

This was the beginnings of my realising that I didn't conform to tradition, I always looked for a better way.

The very thought of the word 'conform' makes me feel uncomfortable. Bert was a conformist; he actually retired on a Tuesday, the day he was sixty-five.

I prefer to push the boundaries. I had a manager who used to say, "if it's not broke, don't fix it". This used to drive me mad. I prefer, "even if something's working well, there must be a better way". That used to drive him mad.

Constant improvement. Not working to other people's times, places, systems or anything, but making your own way.

One more interesting yet sad note about Bert. He retired on his sixty-fifth birthday, looking forward to travelling the world with his wife, from the savings he'd accrued. His wife died six months after he retired. Don't let this be you. Don't conform to the government's idea of retirement – mix in travel or whatever else you want to do, all the way through your life.

## RULES

I've never much liked rules either. I don't like anyone telling me what to do, especially when the rule is stupid, and many are.

I understand there have to be rules to keep society in order, to create the structures we live by, or presumably chaos would prevail. But as a business owner, I've had to push the boundaries a few times, and break many small rules. Why not? There's no rule against it. I'm not saying break the law or act immorally, I'm saying break the rules if you can get an ethical commercial advantage.

I'll give you an example. Many years ago, we tendered for a project to refurbish a leisure centre. The specification called for a certain tiled floor. All the companies had to price for those tiles. We priced for a different tile with the same quality specification, but were half the price.

We were cheaper, but the architect didn't want to accept our tender, because we hadn't allowed the tiles he specified. However, the client, with a saving of several thousands of pounds, appointed us. Had I obeyed the rules, it would have cost us two million pounds' worth of work. We also had the whole project to prove ourselves to the architect.

Never obey silly rules; always find ways to work around them, which give you an advantage, and a better deal for your client.

## SYSTEMS THAT CONTROL OUR LIVES

This is perhaps a little off track, but it has been helpful to me in my life, so I thought I'd pass it on to you.

I grew up in a conventional home, went to a conventional school, had a conventional job, marriage, children. Then I got wise. I realised that religion, the education system, the marriage contract, the days of the week, the hours we work, the age we retire – they are all someone else's idea of how we should live. Handed down from generation to generation.

I don't much care for that. I don't want someone telling me how to live my life. I want to work when I want to work, sleep when I want to sleep. I very much like the idea of building my own life, independent of our systems wherever possible.

There have always been systems that control our lives, mainly by those with power over those without. Now is no exception. In his book, Four, Scott Galloway argues that Amazon, Apple, Facebook and Google could be the new superpowers that control every area of our lives. As Daniel Priestly in his book Key Person of Influence says, nowadays, "you are who Google says you are". The story is yet to unfold on these new systems that control our lives.

# SKILL 14

## COMMUNICATION

I love to communicate, too much some people say. One person with a concept in their head, trying their best to relay that concept, exactly as they mean it to another person, who sees life completely differently. Choosing your words carefully, checking the listener has understood your meaning, then if not, presenting the story in a different way, until you are sure you have been understood. It's very fulfilling when it goes well, frustrating when it doesn't. It's an art.

I've noticed in the companies I've been involved with that mistakes are rife, costing the company hundreds of thousands in lost revenue. In our company, for example, it's not uncommon for deliveries to turn up wrong, orders to be placed wrong, work to be done wrong, tenders to be priced wrong. I could go on. It's massively frustrating, and all avoidable if the person initiating the instruction understood how to communicate.

The goal in communication is to have your meaning or instruction understood. That's difficult, especially as most people are such poor listeners, nodding yes even before you've finished the first sentence. I don't fall for that any more. I push through the yeses, being assertive in my wish to be understood.

Being understood is so difficult because the variables are massive. For starters, we all see life very differently, words mean different things to different people, and most people have made up their mind what you mean before you finish.

Learning styles also play a big part in communication. While an auditory learner could happily listen to you for ages, a visual learner just can't help but butt in, like myself. Years ago, we were taught by a supervisor to communicate information to trades people in three ways: verbally, written, and by drawing a picture. Even then you'll be lucky if they have understood half of what you were communicating.

Let's take a look at this fascinating subject in practice.

## GIVING INSTRUCTIONS

Poor communication will cost your company a fortune, particularly giving poor instructions. It drives me mad when I hear people give instructions, with so little information. I hear things like…

"Pete, could you pop in and price a job tomorrow at 10am? Here's the address."

That's not good communication and will lead to a poor outcome, or at least not the best outcome. You need to set the scene first, with the background to the story. This will give the listener a chance to adjust his thoughts and buy in to your story. It will also make your life easier in the long run, as the listener is armed with all the information they need to do the job properly, without needing to refer back to you. This is how I'd communicate the request…

"Hi Pete, I'd like to give you some background on Jenny, the customer you are going to see tomorrow at 10am. We've been working with her for many years; she is a valued client. She works in the city as a banker, a very switched on lady. She comes across as quiet, but she knows what she wants. She'll be very interested in the detail, so please be over-patient with her. You are due to be there at 10am; please be on time as she's very busy. There is parking outside the property, just ring the bell on the gate when you get there. Hope it goes well, and would you keep me informed?"

Telling a story and setting the scene, giving the whole picture.

## COMMUNICATION CHECKS

As discussed above, when we were young site managers our boss made us communicate to the trades in three ways: verbally, written, and then on a drawing.

We were trained to ask two questions after we had communicated the instruction. The first, "do you understand what you have to do?" to which the answer was almost always yes. Then second, "could you please describe to me what you have to do?". Their description, surprisingly, was nearly always wrong. So we'd have to go through the whole process again until we were 100% sure they had got the right message.

When there was a mistake, my old boss used to say, "it's never the listener's fault, it's always the person giving the instruction". Very true.

I've learned the reason these sorts of mistakes happen is usually down to peer pressure, the pressure to fit-in. It's difficult asking some 6-foot carpenter to repeat back to you what you have just told him, especially as he has almost certainly been nodding yes, all the way through. It could be perceived as a tad patronising, even confrontational. But it's what you need to do to be sure your recipient has got the right message. Stand firm, make him repeat the instruction back to you. It's better to face this, than to have to face the boss because the wall went up in the wrong place.

## GIVE CONTEXT

Similar to setting the scene is giving context. Another thing I've observed from poor communicators is they rarely give context. They just dive into the content and assume you know what they are talking about.

I've had managers walk into my office, when I'm in the middle of something and blurt out a load of stuff about this or that. I often interject with, "I have no idea what you are talking about", even if I do.

When you communicate, even in passing, give context. Give the listener time to drop their existing line of thought and pick up your thread. It's respectful, and leads to better understanding.

For example, imagine you are in the middle of an important email:

> **"Tom, what do you think we should do about the client not paying?"**

If someone interrupted me like that, my usual response would be, "I haven't a clue what you are talking about." A better approach would be:

"Hi Tom, would you have a moment please? You know the London project we are working on? Could I talk to you about the finance, in particular, the issue we are having with non-payment? It's gone way over the due date now."

I always think giving as much context as you can, talking around the issue first with all the relevant background, is respecting the listener, giving them the opportunity to give you a better response, or make a better-quality decision.

I always say to my managers when communicating, assume the person is from Mars, with no knowledge of the subject. Never assume people know what you are talking about – often they are absorbed with thoughts in their own heads.

## EYE CONTACT

An important point in face to face communication, is to make eye contact. If not, you are probably wasting your time.

This is a common theme, and where so many mistakes are made. Assume you are sitting at your computer, head full of words. A colleague walks up behind you and says she'll meet you across the road in the coffee shop at 1pm for lunch, and you nod in agreement.

1pm comes and goes and your colleague returns to ask where you were – she had waited for you all lunch hour. You reply, what! You have no idea what she's talking about. But she swears you agreed to meet her before lunch. You have no recollection of the conversation, because your head never disengaged from the task at hand, and the thought didn't enter your short-term memory.

I think we can all relate to confusion like this, easily avoided if the communicator understood how to communicate. When a person has their head down, they are typically having internal thoughts or feelings. Their senses are focussed internally. The fleeting interruption of your question is not enough to break their chain of thought and place your conversation into their short-term memory.

So, next time you need to communicate something that you want the recipient to remember, wait for them to stop what they are doing, look up into your eyes, and then speak. Wait for a reply, check again, then when you are happy they have truly understood your request, move on.

## PRESENTING TO THE TEAM

One of the things I really love to do is get up in front of my team and announce a new strategy. I find myself delivering with so much passion and energy it surprises me sometimes. I'd certainly believe in me. As leader that's your job, to make people believe in you and your vision.

The key to delivering a great presentation, apart from massive preparation, is to deliver from the heart. If you don't really believe in it, they won't.

Start by giving a wider context and explain why your strategy is an absolute must, and in the interests of everyone. Tell a story, bring people along and deliver with absolute passion.

Now there are certain subtle techniques I've learned which can be useful during your presentation to keep people on side. For example, look for opportunities every now and then to compliment the individuals present, like "Joe's had an amazing year". Also compliment the group with things like "the sales team have really worked hard this year". People love to be praised by the boss in front of their peers, and it keeps your team on-side.

Also give everyone present a reason to believe that your vision will open up opportunities for them in the future, with things like, "there will be plenty of opportunities for those who are interested, if we set up this new division".

Have the financials clearly laid out to support your vision and prove it is viable.

Don't make it too long, no more than an hour, or people will not take it in. Mix in some pictures, figures, text as well as the verbal presentation, to cover all the learning styles present in the room.

Finally, my advice is to go on several public speaking courses. This is an absolute must, a skill you must have to be successful in business. The simple fact is that humans only achieve in groups – if the leader can't communicate his or her vision, they are lost before they have started.

# PART 3:
## DESIGNING AND STARTING YOUR BUSINESS

You've made it through the personal development section and now you have the personal skills to manage people. It's time to learn how to start a business from nothing.

This section is about hard business skills, I'm going to share a step by step process to take you from employee, to business owner, or business owner to bigger business owner.

Like anything else in life, you'll need people to help you, so we start by putting our professional team together.

# SKILL 15

## BUILDING YOUR PROFESSIONAL TEAM

Before you go live with your new business, it's a very good idea to do some preparation. Meet with and appoint your professional team and approach key suppliers to open accounts. Do this well before you start your business. If you already have a team, this will give you a chance to compare my notes with your existing relationships.

You'll need to build relationships with:

> ➤ Accountant
> ➤ Bank manager
> ➤ Solicitor
> ➤ Mentor – Business Advisor
> ➤ Suppliers

### ACCOUNTANT

We'll discuss the accountant in more detail in Skill 32, but here we look at how you find the right one.

While double entry bookkeeping and the way in which accounts are presented are near universal, accountants tend to specialise in particular sectors. Most will have the majority of their client base in one or two sectors. You need one that specialises in your sector.

Generally speaking, small accountancy practices with one or two partners, will deal with smaller firms, and their charges will be in proportion. However, you shouldn't make your choice of accountant on cost alone. A smaller practice will probably be busy, and difficult to get hold of when you need them.

If you intend to grow your business, you need a larger practice. One that can take you from start-up right through. Changing accountants can be a painful experience, as they hold a lot of information the next accountant will need, and in my experience, they are sometimes not that forthcoming in providing that information for the new accountant.

A good place to start to find an accountant is by asking people you know who are in business, in your sector. If you don't know anyone, source some appropriate networking events. If this doesn't bear fruit, google some local accountants.

First, check out their website and get a feel for the business and the sectors in which they specialise, then make a call. Don't email, you want to see how friendly they are towards you on the phone. Ask to speak with the accountant, explain you are about to start a business and need an accountant. Gauge the reaction: you want an accountant motivated to help you get started and grow with you.

Arrange a meeting. Go to their offices to assess the size of the practice. Take note of how long they keep you waiting. Listen to how the receptionist deals with calls, take it all in. Go prepared with a list of questions such as the following:

> What sectors do you specialise in?
> How many companies do you personally look after?
> What services do you offer other than year-end accounts?
> How many partners and support staff are there at the firm?
> How long on average does it take you to return calls?
> How experienced are you in tax matters?
> What is your cost structure?

Take notes of their answers for later comparison. One note here, expect positive answers to all your questions. The standard line is, "we'll save you our fees in tax in the first year". They won't. You'll only really know how much they add value after you work with them for a whole financial year, and you can always change after that.

When you have interviewed a few accountants, you'll begin to get a feel for the best person for you, and that is the most important thing. You have to feel you can call your accountant any time, and get a friendly greeting, not a standoffish voice on the end of the phone.

Lastly, choose a person you feel comfortable talking with.

## BANK MANAGER

Once you or your accountant has formed the new company at Companies House, a very simple and inexpensive process done online, you need to open your business bank accounts, two of them, a current and a high interest account. Any of the high street banks are much the same. It's a good idea to open accounts with two banks and use one as a reserve account. This way you'll build up a history with both, should you ever need to change your primary account.

The person you need to book an appointment with is the business banking manager. Barclays call their managers 'relationship managers', other banks do differently. Like accountants, banks dedicate their managers to certain sectors, so they can build expertise and serve the sector better.

Go to the meeting prepared. Take information about the business, expected turnover in years one, two and three, to give the manager a good feel for your business. Take a business plan if you have one. Business plans are a whole topic on their own, and most of the content can be obtained from this book. I've prepared some examples for you on the book website: *www.carmelcresttraining.com/50skills*

If you need an overdraft, you will not get one without security. Banks love security, usually taking first charge over your home or another property; they will also ask you for a company and personal debenture, giving them first charge over all you own and all the company book debts.

I hope you have an understanding partner. My home was used as security for many years, and it was the first thing I had removed as soon as I had built up enough equity.

Please always keep the following in mind when dealing with your bank and you won't go far wrong. Banks want to know one thing:

How will we get our money back if it goes wrong?

Satisfy that criteria, and they'll lend you anything, generally. They'll also want you to have what has become known as 'some skin in the deal'. In other words, they want you to put your money where your mouth is. That way they know you are serious about making this work.

My manager once said to me, that he lends to me, not the business. In other words, the trust is in me, as a trusted custodian of the business. I don't know whether that's true or not, but I do know that the relationship you have with your manager is very important indeed. I have been able to secure a lot of short-term money over the phone in the past, because he trusts what I say.

This can only be built up over time, with contact. Most people only speak to their manager when they call every year, asking for a meeting. Never do that. Call him or her at least once a month, keep them in the loop, explain how the firm is doing and what your future plans are. Involve them in your business.

Your manager will want to know that you understand business, particularly the financials. They will want to know you are in control. They will expect you to know what your monthly turnover, gross profit, net profit, overheads and expected future sales are, and if not asked directly, you should drop this into conversation. Do not meet with the manager unless you know your figures, or you'll be wasting your time.

Another important point in dealing with the bank is to give them an early warning of problems. If your cash flow is likely to suffer in a month's time, for one month or so, call the manager and tell him or her. When it happens there will be no surprise, and they will know you are on top of the business and may even suggest you take a further overdraft, short-term.

Learn financial skills 32-42 before going to see the bank manager.

One more thing. Opening an account these days is a lengthy and bureaucratic process. Money laundering laws have added layers of paperwork to the process. We have just opened an account with Barclays that took over three months.

## LEGAL TEAM

You need two types of legal advice, a good general practice legal firm, and a contract law specialist, who may be part of the same firm depending on the size. Also, depending on your specialism, specialist advice such as property conveyancing.

Luckily, I've not had too many dealings with solicitors over the years, apart from property purchases and I hope you don't either, as they are very expensive. I've been sued at an industrial tribunal a couple of times, and I've needed contract law advice many times.

My advice here is to get the biggest firm you can afford, and it won't be cheap.

It's a good idea to call and make an appointment to meet with the practice manager, if they have one. When you meet, discuss your new venture and how they could help in future. The purpose of the meeting is to begin the relationship, so when you do need help, you have a contact.

You'll need them in the early days, as I'd strongly advise you to have them cast their eye over your employment contracts and various other contracts you may enter into. The investment will be worth it.

I'll just diversify here for a moment to discuss a couple of legal cases I've been wrapped up in that may help you.

I have a certain approach to litigation, which I'll illustrate by sharing a story of something that happened to me many years ago.

A bookkeeper stole £24,000 from us over a four-year period. Of course, we let her go, writing off the money. A few months later she brazenly took us to an industrial tribunal for wrongful dismissal and of course, she lost.

This time, we started proceedings against her to recover our money, plus costs. But when I asked the solicitor for a cost estimate, she said around £20,000, and that's not including the time it would take us to prepare for the court case, and the stress it would cause. After consideration, we let it go.

I've taken that stance several times in business. Once when a client refused to pay a final account of £60,000 just because they were a large company and could. We threatened court action, there response was, 'fine, take us to court'. Another time when a client had refused to pay us for additional work they had asked for. When I looked into it, on both occasions, I came to the conclusion that it was not worth the emotional stress and further financial risk. So I decided not to take action.

I thought our time would be much better spent improving our systems to prevent big mistakes as I call them (see Skill 46 for more information on mistakes).

In all these cases, people around me insisted I get justice, even my family. But my stance is this: I don't want anything to detract from my focus on building my business. If so, then they have won another battle. I always let it go, bear no malice, and push on.

There is only one exception to this where I would go all the way: when it was a matter of reputation. This is worth protecting at all costs. Luckily, I've never been in that position.

## MENTOR - BUSINESS ADVISOR

You would be very wise to seek out a person who has done what you want to do, and is willing to advise you. But it is unlikely you'll find anyone. People like that are either still doing it themselves or enjoying the spoils of their labours on a beach, or writing a book like me. But do try first.

If not, try mixing with business people at say the golf or tennis club, or at a networking event. But if you can't find someone who has actually done what you want to do, find a good business advisor.

These are usually ex business people or people who have technical business skills, and have worked with many companies. Their experience is invaluable. They are able to give insight into the way other businesses are run, and that can give you some good ideas.

They will usually have a specialism of their own, such as financial, or strategy. So, choose one that complements your own skills and personality – you don't want just another you, but a different viewpoint. John Trueman, my long-standing advisor, is somewhat of a pessimist, I'm sure he won't mind me saying; he has a very careful approach to life, whilst I'm raring to go full speed ahead with very little information or diligence.

The most important thing about working with an advisor is that you get on with each other. You may not see life the same way, but you get on, trust and respect each other.

Your advisor will probably become your friend, as I have with John, and you should be as open with them as you are with your partner. It's the only way they can truly help; they need to know your plans, finances, everything.

It can be expensive working with an advisor, and you have to give up your time when you are sometimes busy. I have found that most of the times I meet with John, we discuss subjects I'm already aware of, but are nevertheless interesting. However, on occasions, he may mention something, even in passing, that has a massive influence on me, and in fact changes the course of my business, and sometimes life, for the good. That one line is worth all the fee, and this is the benefit of working with an advisor.

One more thing. You should be so open with your advisor that when you outgrow him or her, and you probably will, you have an open conversation about finding a new advisor.

## SUPPLIERS

Setting up accounts with suppliers before you start out is a great idea. Good credit is essential to ensure good cash flow (see Skill 37).

Work out who your main suppliers will be. Contact them and ask to meet the area rep for a chat about your ideas, and how you can work together in future. Suppliers will normally want to see three years' worth of good accounts to give you credit, so you'll have to persuade them that you are worth the risk. They will usually want the first few payments to be in cash, until they trust you. Then if you are lucky, they may give you a small amount of credit to start you off.

One note on this. I hope you have a good credit history and rating. Because you are going to need that to get any credit these days. If not, work on that before you start the business.

Generally, smaller companies, where the owner has the say, will allow you a small credit limit; with larger companies it will be a tick box exercise, and it's unlikely you'll get credit. In any case ask to speak with the area rep, they will listen to your story, and they may persuade head office to set up a small credit line if they like you and trust in what you say. It's well worth trying, as the alternative is to pay cash, and we never, ever, pay cash in business, unless we are forced to; we always set up accounts.

If so, ask for 90 days' credit – you won't get it but ask anyway. Then 60, try 45 and as a last resort, settle on 30 days' credit, never under. The aim is to get better terms than you are giving your clients. Cash flow is king.

# SKILL 16

## THE PLANNING PROCESS

Now you are prepared and ready to go, it's time to begin planning your business. Notice I said planning, not diving in. That'd be like setting off to sea with no destination.

But first, let's be clear what the term 'planning', and the planning process actually is.

What does the term planning mean to you? In my experience, it means different things to different people. It's one of those throwaway words we all know what it means, but not really. Let me clear this up for you.

Planning is the generic term for a three-part process, which starts with an idea you turn into a goal. From the goal, you create a vision, and lastly you plan the steps you need to take to achieve your vision, known as the action plan, as follows:

- ➢ Step 1. Goal setting - The idea becomes a goal.
- ➢ Step 2. Vision – Putting meat on the bone of your goal.
- ➢ Step 3. Action Planning – Planning the actions you need to take to achieve your vision.

Thus, during daily planning time, you could be engaged in any of the above.

## WHY YOU SHOULD PLAN

Napoleon Hill in Think and Grow Rich says that, "people do not become rich, simply because they never give any deep thought to the matter", they just live, day by day, doing the same thing. It's as simple as that. What you think about and where you focus your energy, tends to happen. If you never focus your energy on a meaningful goal, nowhere is where you will go.

I've learned to set goals and make plans for every area of my life, including my personal life. My partner and I go away for a long weekend in early January to plan. We plan the life we want in the coming year, rather than leaving it to chance. We agree things like theatre trips, weekends away, holidays, and time with family.

We don't see this process as restrictive, we see it as giving us the life that makes us happy. If something better comes up, or we need to change it, then we do.

Let's think about the implications for you and your family of not planning.

## DON'T BE SOMEONE ELSE'S PLAN

Jim Rohn, the famous personal development speaker, said:

> "If you don't design your own life plan, chances are you'll fall into someone else's plan. And guess what they have planned for you? Not much."

I know this to be true. I have planned the lives of hundreds of people to suit my business. That has involved changes in their work location, job roles, pay and hours. The truth is, as an employee you are at the whim of your boss.

I'm not saying all bosses are bad – some have your interests at heart, as we do in our businesses. But at the end of the day, if the business takes a nose-dive, your boss will sometimes have no choice but to make cut-backs.

## AUTONOMY

Do you remember at school putting your hand up to use the loo? Well in some ways it's no different in some workplaces today. Most employees have to ask for a couple of hours off to go see their child in the nativity, or go to the dentist.

I don't know about you, but I don't want to have to tell my wife, the boss wouldn't let me come see our son in the nativity. In my world, that's not quality of life; in fact, it makes me very uncomfortable. Freedom of choice has been a major driver in my life.

## ALWAYS DOING WHAT YOU'VE ALWAYS DONE

"If you always do what you've always done, you'll always get what you've always got."

This anonymous famous quote illustrates clearly what you get if you do not set goals to do something different.

Millions of people live and work in systems designed to encourage us to act like everyone else. The typical worker goes through the education system, into the employment system until retirement. Doing what everyone else does.

It doesn't have to be this way. You can design your own life, you really can. Set yourself goals, put meat on the bones of those goals in your vision, then plan the steps you need to take to get there in your action plan. It's the only way to change your life.

I hope I have got you thinking about the implications of not planning, and I've given you a good reason to start.

## I DON'T JUST MEAN BUSINESS

I'm not just talking about planning in the business context. I mentioned in Skill 1 the importance of balance to your success and how all areas of your life are all interrelated. To reiterate, you can never achieve true wealth by pursuing money alone, you need to set goals and plan towards:

- ➢ Good diet.
- ➢ Daily exercise.
- ➢ Time with those you are in key relationships with, especially your partner.
- ➢ Business – money.

Some practical tips for the planning process:

- ➢ Make planning a priority part of your day.
- ➢ Plan at the same time of day, morning or evening; repetition is key, it must become a habit.
- ➢ Plan every area of your life not just business, but also diet,

exercise, time with loved ones, and business. Everything has to be in balance.

Now we are clear on the process, we are going to take a deeper look at each area in turn: goal setting, vision and finally action planning.

# SKILL 17

## GOAL SETTING

You may have had the idea of developing yourself, starting your own business or growing your existing business for some while. But nothing will change unless you put a stake in the ground, and make the decision to do it.

### STRONG GOALS GIVE YOU A PURPOSE

If you think about it, a goal gives you a purpose. Simon Sinek in Start with Why, explains the importance of having a big why, a purpose in life. Having a clear purpose pulls you through the difficult times. It gives you the motivation to get out of bed, take action, and face the difficult decisions.

The more passionate you are about achieving your goals, the more likely you are to get through any tough times. The weaker your goal, the more likely you are to be distracted and drop the goal.

Without strong goals, you are prey to all sorts of negativity, not just from other people but your own thoughts, boredom and lethargy. Strong goals will immunise you from negativity.

Try it now. Think of a goal that is just outside your reach that could alter you, and your family's life.

It feels a little scary, and exciting, doesn't it? You'll need to keep your focus to achieve that goal, and that's what you want, a goal big enough to keep you focussed, and away from the telly.

## BIG OR SMALL GOALS

There are different schools of thought on goals. Some think you should set small achievable goals, within your comfort zone. Some say set big goals you have no idea how you will reach. For example, don't think local company, think national, or even global.

Here's a couple of suggestions from famous people about goal setting. Steve Garvey was a famous American Baseball player; he thought you should set goals that are almost out of reach. "If you set a goal that is attainable without much work or thought, you are stuck with something below your true talent and potential."

It has to be remembered that Steve went broke after he stopped playing, but I like his take on goals.

I also particularly like Steve Jobs' take on goals. He famously said:

> "You can't connect the dots looking forward; you can only connect them looking backward. So you have to trust that the dots will somehow connect in your future. You have to trust in something – your gut, destiny, life, karma, whatever."

I love this. It reminds me of when I climb mountains. I look up and have very little idea how I'm going to get to the top. I just take one step at a time.

Looking back over my life, although I have goals years into the future, I have always known what steps I needed to take to achieve them. Had I read Steve's quote in my twenties, I think I'd have set bigger goals, and joined the dots as I went along. I always try to now, and I would encourage you to do the same.

I will put one caveat in here. There have been times when I've pushed myself a little too much. These are the times when I lay awake at night stressing. At these times, I mostly back away from the deal I was about to do or reduce my goal. I think in reality we all have different levels of stress we can handle, and you don't want to be the richest man or woman in the cemetery, you want a balanced, happy, long life.

# SKILL 18

## VISION

You've made the decision to pursue a meaningful goal, start or grow a company. Fine, but it's all in your head. What does that really look like?

It's time to put your thoughts to paper and put some meat on the bones of that goal and create the vision. That way you'll head off in the right direction and know exactly what steps to take to get there.

This process involves imagining your business in the future, in as much detail as you can, and writing it down, which will force you to think it through.

Paint a written picture of your business. What does it look and feel like, what are your colours, what product or service do you provide, who are the staff and what does it feel like working at your firm?

A good way to do this is to imagine that you are going to franchise the business at some stage. You'll need to explain every detail of your business to other people. This needs to be very detailed.

Find yourself somewhere quiet, with your business partner if you have one, and put deep thought into imagining what your business will look like in say two-five years from now.

You are beginning to create your future in your head and on paper, so make it as real as possible. The more detailed you can be the more chance of it becoming real.

You could consider:

> ➤ Where will your office be situated?
> ➤ What will it look like?
> ➤ What colours will it be?
> ➤ What feel will it have?
> ➤ What will the employees be like and how many?
> ➤ What will the turnover be?
> ➤ What will gross and net profits be?
> ➤ Geographically, where will you trade?
> ➤ What values will you have?
> ➤ What sort of quality do you want to provide?

## THE SERVICE OR PRODUCT

Once you are clear on the look and feel of your business, move on to consider what problem your business will be solving and how will the business serve others. What is the service or product? How will you provide a better service than competitors?

It will help others understand your business if you keep it simple. You really need to be able to explain your business in a sentence or two. For example:

> "We provide high quality construction services to
> the Health, Education, and Leisure sectors."

When you are clear about your service, go on to think about the values you want for the business.

## VALUES

What values do you want for your company? Honesty and integrity, for example – how do you want staff to treat each other? Fairly and equally? This is your chance to design your culture, before you take your service to the market. Read Skill 23 for guidance with values.

## VISION STATEMENT

When you've completed the above steps, you will have created your vision statement. This forms the blueprint for your new business. A very exciting stage to reach. Like a set of plans for a house, all that is stopping this design from actually existing is time, action and effort.

The vision statement is often summarised into a few concise sentences, which are shown to the world on your website. This is the 'Vision Statement Summary', often confused with the vision statement.

For example:

> "To provide trusted property investment opportunities
> to investors who want 8% plus return."

Decide on your vision statement summary.

## A STAKE IN THE GROUND

At this point it is getting exciting. When you complete this exercise, you have put a stake in the ground at some point in the future. This is crucial; you now have a clear goal and vision of where you are going. The next thing you'll need is a plan to get you there.

# SKILL 19

## ACTION PLANNING

Now your vision is clear, the next stage is to work out how you are going to make it a reality, what actions do you need to take?

This is called action planning. The action plan is the document that manages the logical steps toward your vision, it organises and provokes you to take action in a logical sequence.

As Antoine de Saint-Exupéry said, in his famous quote: "A goal without a plan, is just a wish."

Whether you are starting a new business or growing your existing one, the process I've developed is the same:

1. Think about where you are right now.
2. Think about the vision of your new company.
3. Identify the gaps, and what action you need to take to get there.

Yes, it is that simple!

This is actually the Investors in People (IIP) process, but IIP relates specifically to gaps in people skills, and those gaps become the individual's training plans.

However, you are concerned with more than just people skill gaps, you have to assess what every area of the business will need to meet your vision. For example:

> ➤ Recruiting and training new staff or training existing staff.
> ➤ Writing new or improving existing systems.
> ➤ Raising additional finance.
> ➤ Finding new premises.
> ➤ Branding or rebranding.
> ➤ Sales and marketing.
> ➤ Timescales for all this to happen.

You can find examples of action plans I've prepared for you at the book website *www.carmelcresttraining.com/50skills*

One last thing on planning. This is your time to make your future better, it's serious time and it needs to be prioritised over other activities. Television and activities which detract you from the plan are a thing of the past.

# SKILL 20

## ORGANISATION CHART

Now things are getting really exciting. You have your goal, vision and action plan. You have relationships in place with your professional team, the company is formed at Companies House, and the bank accounts are open.

But there's more to do before you start trading. Some detailed planning needs to take place, and the first component is your organisational chart, sometimes referred to as company structure. It's your map of the business.

It serves the following functions:

> ➤ It helps you organise the business into departments.
> ➤ It helps you define the job roles within those departments.
> ➤ It can define lines of communication and authority.

Like the one below, you can see that they are set out into departments. Typically, a business would be structured as follows:

> ➤ Operations – your product or service.
> ➤ Sales and marketing.
> ➤ Finance.

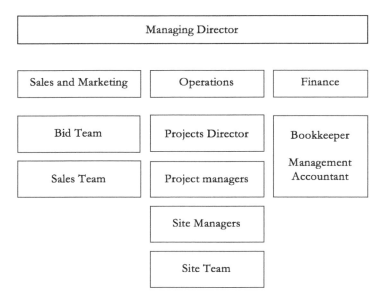

This is an example of a traditional business structure, but yours doesn't have to fit this model – it can be set out any way you want.

Some roles, such as administration, a support role, don't fit well into any department, but tend to serve all of them. These anomalies usually sit under the operations department.

Operations is usually far bigger than any other department, as this is the product or service. There are usually more layers here. In construction, for example, there is a hierarchy of authority. Typically, project managers, site managers, supervisors and so on.

Notice that IT and HR are placed under finance, but these could equally be placed under separate departments.

## FLAT STRUCTURES

By flat I mean not too many layers of authority. As the company grows, the structure tends to move out sideways, rather than downwards with more layers of authority. Information is more easily disseminated in flat structures, for example, when implementing new policies or strategies. It will also enable you to act quickly in times of change.

Take time to think about who is needed in what role in your business. You should end up with departments and the name of the role defined in each box under the department heading.

If you know the name of the person carrying out the role, put it in the box. In the early days your name could appear in many of the boxes, but as you grow, the role can be filled by someone else.

In fact, it is essential from the outset, you plan yourself out of the business in the long-run. Michael Gerber in The E-Myth, his amazing book on systemising businesses, said, "your aim is to work on, not in, the business". You are an entrepreneur, not a manager. More about exit routes in Skill 31.

Now consider how you will you structure your business.

I've prepared some examples for you at the book website *www.carmelcresttraining.com/50skills*

# SKILL 21

## JOB ROLES

You have hopefully given a lot of thought to how you want your business structured. Defined the departments and have the name of the job role in each box. You now have a map of your business.

You've done amazing to get this far, and now you need to think through the job roles: what does each person do?

### WRITING THE JOB ROLES

Your structure is a series of boxes with the name of the job role shown. Pick one. Imagine the small box blown up to A4. Write the name of the job role at the top of the page.

Now think through what the role will consist of, and bullet point the duties. Keep this brief and general, no detail for now; also, keep to one page of A4. In my experience, anymore and it won't happen.

Don't concern yourself with prioritising the task yet either. The objective is for you to think through the role and ask yourself, what do I want the person carrying out that role to do?

Your mind set at this point is, "what", do I want done. Not, "how" do I want it done.

Here's an example of a job role for the project manager above:

## PROJECT MANAGER (PM)

**Role overview:**
As PM you are solely responsible for the day-to-day running of every aspect of site operations, including compliance with the contract documents, quality, health and safety, profit, client and staff care.

Key responsibilities include:

> ➢ Working in accordance with contract documents
> ➢ Preparation of programmes
> ➢ Measurement and submission of variations and instructions
> ➢ Measurement of valuations
> ➢ Attending site progress meetings
> ➢ Attend pre-start meetings
> ➢ H&S management on site
> ➢ Preparation of site waste management plans
> ➢ Measure materials and orders materials
> ➢ Organise site operations
> ➢ Manage labour and sub-contractors
> ➢ Site planning

Carry out this operation for every role on your structure, including you own. Re-work them until you are happy that every function that has to be carried out, is allocated. Leave no stone unturned.

Only then do we consider "how" things are carried out.

# SKILL 22

## SYSTEMS AND PROCESSES

Now we are going deep into my favourite area. My old manager used to call me Mr System, for good reason. I had a system for everything.

Up to this point, all the planning has centred around "what" your business and staff are going to do. Your thought process changes at this point, to "how" your staff are going to carry out the task. This involves writing a system for that task.

Writing the systems can be a lengthy process but well worth the time. It will enable you to make your mistakes on paper, rather than in practice.

A good example to follow, is that of the franchise model. Their strength lies in their detailed systems. At some point, someone has given deep thought to how the whole business will work, and written down every tiny component. Even down to how many times you will allow the phone to ring before being answered. These are your systems and processes.

But before we get into writing your systems and processes, I want you to be clear, what system processes are:

## SYSTEMS AND PROCESSES

To explain the difference. In our firm, we have an accounts process and a tender bidding process. These processes are made up of many systems. I hope that explained it.

When my father left our business to me, we had very few systems. It frustrated me that I had no way of managing the building sites from the office, and no way of maintaining quality across the company, unless I went to the site to see for myself.

I searched for ways of systemising my business to get more control back in the office, and along with Michael Gerber's E Myth, I discovered the ISO 9001 quality management system.

I attended a five-day training programme at the British Standard Institute's headquarters in Milton Keynes, and learned about processes and systems.

I returned to the company a man on a mission. I sought out a consultant, and during the next few months we thought through how we wanted every minute detail of the company to be carried out. We wrote the book, that 'was' the business, and I knew my company inside out. They call this the quality manual, the book of systems.

This book is the datum document from which every future change is made.

## SYSTEMS VS BRAINS

The more you systemise your business, the less brain power and human intervention you need. The more you systemise, the less your wage bill will be, generally. People and brains cost money.

Wherever I can, I install a system to minimise human input. In my businesses, operating in construction and property, full systemisation is not always possible (yet!), but where I can I do.

Our accounts department, for example, was top heavy with staff mainly because of the amount of monthly management information I required, which had to be carried out manually. We invested over £40,000 in new software, and now we have the information at our fingertip.

The best example I can give of a great system is McDonald's. Ray Croc discussed in his book, Grinding it Out, how his research and development department spent weeks systemising every tiny detail of the process. As we know, this has resulted in the massive franchise model company we know today. The fact that they can employ unskilled, inexpensive labour to carry out such technical tasks is testament to the amazing systems they employ.

The franchise model is a good one to aim for in all businesses. You should be able to write your business down in a book, so that someone else could replicate it in another city. That's how detailed it should be. I've already mentioned Michael Gerber's The E Myth, and I know no better book on systemising than this.

## SYSTEMS VS AUTONOMY

The rule of thumb in business, is the more you systemise, the less autonomy your staff have. The system takes away the need to think, to some degree.

With certain people, this leads to frustration, but others like not having to think for themselves.

With this in mind, when you create the system, be mindful of the type of person who will be carrying out the role. For example, never try to systemise sales people, or you'll have none. They are free spirited souls, and need freedom.

Systemisation is a balance between organising the company's processes, and giving space for creativity. Generally speaking, senior staff involved in strategy need space to be creative and try out new ideas, as do those involved in creative professions, so allow more flexibility here. But where the job requires repetition, some degree of systemisation will be essential.

That said, nearly all processes in your business will require some systemisation as you grow, particularly the financial process. This is essential to provide a framework for staff to carry out day to day operations.

Systems should make people's lives easier. One leading hospital we work for introduced, in their words, 'land breaking' software, where five signatures are required to authorise a payment to their suppliers. That's bureaucracy, not streamlining; do not get carried away and over complicate your systems. You know by now I'm all about simplicity.

Some systems can be very simple and require little training, maybe just a conversation; some are more complex and require detailed written instruction, media or verbal training. All systems must be in writing.

## WRITING THE SYSTEMS

Where do you start?

You start at the beginning and follow through to the end. Yes, it's that obvious.

Take one job role at a time, and one task on that job role at a time. Now expand that task and create the system. Tell that staff member how you want that task carried out.

I call this 'process analysis'. You analyse the process from inception, to completion. Then reduce and reduce to the absolute minimum.

Take an ordering process, for example. It has a start, presumably someone needs something ordering, and it has a finish, where the goods are delivered.

Start = Thought                          End = Goods Delivered

Now fill in the gaps with the steps required. You need to think through and produce a flow diagram of the complete process, stage by stage. For example, this process could be something like:

> ➢ Goods required, quantified on a materials requisition sheet.
> ➢ Materials requisition emailed to three suppliers.

- ➢ Supplier quotes returned.
- ➢ Carry out analysis of quotes.
- ➢ Select least expensive (unless there is good reason).
- ➢ Send instruction to the office to place order.
- ➢ Goods delivered.
- ➢ Goods checked.

You are designing your business piece by piece.

If you are improving an existing system, process out exactly how it is currently carried out. Consider what isn't working well and what is. Ask yourself, are there any duplications in the current system? There often is. Duplications are opportunities for error, so remove them.

I have examples of several systems for you on the book website, at *www.carmelcresttraining.com/50skills*

I rarely list out like I have above, I use either A3 paper, a flip chart, sticky notes or occasionally a Word document.

Once you have the process laid out end to end. Look at it again with a critical eye. Consult the people who will be using the process, and take their comments on board. Amend the process to reduce duplications and minimise, minimise more, until it's as short and efficient as possible. This is where you make labour savings.

Do this for every bullet point on that job role, then move on to the next role.

Remember, some processes will be very short, such as, 'the phone is to be answered within three rings'. A polite greeting must follow such as, "good morning, this is A. Brown & Co, how can I help today?".

Some will be very detailed, such as that for ordering material. It matters not, every function needs a system, so be thorough.

Once you are happy that this is the shortest and most efficient route from A to B, make it look pretty and head it with the name of the process. That's one page in your book of processes.

This will take some time to complete, but is well worth doing. As I said, make your mistakes on paper and in your head, rather than in real life.

You will end up with the following:

- ➢ A company structure.
- ➢ Job roles.
- ➢ Systems for each job role.

# SKILL 23

## CULTURE

Now you've clearly defined what your business will do and how you will do it, it's time to focus on a less tangible and often overlooked, but equally important area: the culture of your business.

Your business is not complete before you are clear about what sort of culture you want. Culture refers to the values of the business, and as I said previously, your personal values will create the culture for your business.

Your first task is to give some thought, and be clear about what your values are. In my experience, not many people ever give this the thought it deserves. If you're not clear about how to act at work, your staff won't be either.

Here's some important values to me:

- ➤ Doing what I say I will do
- ➤ Honesty
- ➤ Trust
- ➤ Respect for others
- ➤ Openness

These are important to me as a person, so they inevitably extended to my business.

It's extremely important to get this right. It will determine the standards for your business, and the feel of your business too. The world will judge you by these values. Your values will also serve to guide your team, so they understand what is and isn't acceptable at the firm, how to treat your clients and one another.

The owner creates the culture; the team follow. If there are no values, you've only yourself to blame if it goes wrong, and it will.

Here is an example of a company where the owner either hasn't defined the culture, or hasn't communicated it to the team.

My son Alex and I visited a bathroom supplier a few weeks ago to select bathrooms for our properties. We stood in the reception before a gentleman who, without lifting his head, said, "what can I do for ya", in an abrupt voice. I asked if there was a showroom, to which he grunted "no, not here".

As we turned to walk out, a female sales assistant spoke out: "Excuse me, we don't have a showroom here but we do at our Cambridge branch. Is there something I can help you with?"

We walked back and began a conversation, which led to us ordering a lot of bathrooms and an ongoing relationship.

As we walked out, I turned to my son and said, "Now that's a great example of a company where there is no clear culture, and if there is, it isn't being communicated down to the shop floor."

## WHY DO WE NEED A CULTURE?

The culture sets the tone for your business, so employees understand what is acceptable and what is not, including:

- ➤ What type of person to recruit
- ➤ How to act at your firm
- ➤ What is important to the company
- ➤ How to treat clients and customers
- ➤ How to treat each other
- ➤ What decisions to make in a given circumstance

## WHERE DO YOU START

There is no set way to write a culture document. The key thing is to spend time thinking about what is important to you, and get it down on paper.

It can be generalised statements like, we value honesty. Or better still it can go on to define what that means in your business. Search Google for culture statements – you'll find many examples.

The important thing is that you've given this thought and have one.

# SKILL 24

## IMPLEMENTATION

You now have all you need to start your business, it's just a case of when's the right time, and only you know that.

The best time will probably be when you have sufficient funds to carry you over for at least one to two years to be safe. Also, when you have clients willing to give you work.

You will likely be putting in all hours in the first year, so ensure your family understand the situation, as their support will be essential.

Soon, hopefully, you'll be recruiting staff, and your processes and systems will kick-in. That's when the fun starts.

One point before we discuss implementation. If you are leaving your current employer to start up in business, maybe as a competitor, have the balls to be honest with your boss about your intentions, not like my old manager Dick. You'll be surprised. Business owners are seldom vindictive people – it's why they got where they are. They'll often help you on your way and you can work together in the future. You don't want to start out with enemies.

## GOING LIVE

You've sat in your office for weeks, writing and re-writing the systems, and you are very happy with the outcome. Only one problem: you are the only one who knows about it.

One thing I've learned in business, is that many great ideas fall down at implementation stage, and this has been a weakness of mine over the years.

Why? I hear you ask.

I've found there are two main reasons:

> ➤ Lack of training
> ➤ Lack of buy-in

## TRAINING

In the early days, I underestimated the amount of training that would be required to bring a new recruit up-to-speed. What may be very clear in your head, means nothing to a new recruit. You need to be patient and train your staff in their job role, and patience you will need in abundance.

Some people think that as soon as a new member of staff starts, their life will become easier. It won't. On the contrary, in the first few weeks this will definitely increase your workload, so be ready for that. But as their learning and experience grow, your life should become easier.

Or, as is sometimes the case, you spend two weeks training them and one of two things happens. They either leave, because they don't like or can't do the job, or you sack them because you know they are never going to get it. Either way, you have just wasted two weeks of your life. Welcome to running a business.

On the up side: when this happens a few times, as I'm sure it will, your interview skills suddenly improve drastically.

Training is a subject all of its own, but generally, if you assume the trainee is from Mars, you won't go far wrong.

## BUY-IN

If you already have a business and want to implement a new system, your system will have much more chance of success if you can get staff buy-in.

The young and naive me used to write new system from my comfortable office and get very excited. Then I'd call a meeting with my staff to announce the new system.

My PowerPoints were impeccable, I always thought I'd communicated the idea very well, taking account of all the different learning styles in the room. I was sure they understood how it worked, because they were all nodding in agreement.

In my mind, that was a done deal. My work here was done. Monday morning the system would be in operation.

Then, come Monday morning, to my frustration nothing changed, and to my further frustration, nothing changed for weeks. I'm not sure they even remembered the new system. This happened time and time again, until the penny dropped.

I learned that imposing my ideas onto staff was never going to work. Where I was creating something that would change the working lives of the team, it was definitely time to involve the team from the outset.

I learned to get their input from day-one. Then incorporate as many of their ideas as possible. I learned that if the system was partly their idea, they tried harder to make it work.

I further learned that if I delegated the entire task of coming up with the new system, I found this worked even better. They worked extra hard to make it work, as it was their system and not mine, and the bonus was freeing up my time.

So, in summary, never impose an idea on your staff, always consult and incorporate their ideas, or delegate the whole thing.

## ASSIGN RESPONSIBILITY

One last technique I've found useful when implementing a new system, is appointing a champion to make sure the system is adopted by all the staff in the company.

Making someone responsible has several advantages. It saves you going around to staff moaning, and you have a single point of contact to keep up to date with progress.

# SKILL 25

## THINGS YOU NEED TO MEASURE

Hopefully you are now in business, staff trained and things are busy. Statistically, you are in a very vulnerable place right now. You need to keep your eye on the ball, and part of that is to measure key areas of the business – these are your key performance indicators, KPIs.

I can't tell you how many businesses I've seen go under because they don't measure the critical things. Many small businesses don't measure anything, apart from what they have in the bank.

A company going under can be likened to a ship taking on water very slowly. You'd hardly notice it for a time, everything's working ok, but it's a few centimetres lower in the water every day. Until that critical point of no return, and the ship sinks.

It's the same in businesses. On the surface, it seems like business as usual. But if you have no way of knowing how much money you are making, you could be going under day by day, without even knowing it. So it's essential to identify the key areas that are so critical to your survival and success.

What are these?

Deborah Meaden, in her book Common Sense Rules, said there are only a few things that are important to your business. I agree, and those things need measuring. You could probably fit these on one, maybe two hands. In my experience, if you have a long list of things to measure, you won't bother. Like all things in business, keep it simple and relevant.

A google search for business KPIs reveals tens of ideas, but I'm interested in you learning only what you MUST measure. If you do this you'll have a good chance of making it through the first few years in business.

So, you must have a process in place for measuring the following:

> Monthly sales
> Cash Flow (Creditors and Debtors – Skill 38)
> Gross Profit (Skill 33)
> Overheads (Skill 34)
> Work in Progress (Skill 40)
> Client Satisfaction

Set target KPIs for the above, and have a system for measuring that target at least monthly, preferably weekly. Let's examine the sort of targets you should be looking at below. I discuss budgeting in Skill 42.

## MONTHLY SALES

This should be very easy to measure: simply add up all the sales invoices that month.

The target should be:

➤ As per your monthly budget (Skill 42)

## CASH FLOW

As discussed in Skill 37, cash flow is the time it takes from when you invoice, to the money landing in your bank. This is known as debtor days, and you should always know your average debtor days.

The target should be:

➤ Invoice the day the job completes (not monthly).
➤ Paid on or before what is stated in your credit terms.

Employ a great credit controller, preferably in-house.

## GROSS PROFIT

The profit you earn before overheads, discussed in Skill 33.

The target should be:

➤ Whatever percentage you have priced in your budget.

## OVERHEADS

Your running costs and costs not attributed to a project, discussed in Skill 34.

The target should be:

> ➤ Whatever percentage you have budgeted for.

But also have a complete list of these and check regularly.

## WORK IN PROGRESS (WIP)

One of the main reasons it's so difficult for some companies to identify how they are performing financially, is down to poor work-in-progress information. WIP, discussed in Skill 40, is the work you have in the system, not yet invoiced. Neither have you been invoiced by suppliers.

Not knowing your WIP is dangerous. It can seriously out-balance the figures, and you won't know where you are financially. That is a dangerous and scary place to be.

Many businesses go under because of poor profit coupled with poor WIP management. You need to know how much your WIP is every month, or you could be running the risk of insolvency.

Thousands of business fall foul to this. Companies House statistics reveal that eight out of ten businesses fail in the first year, and four out of ten in the first five years. I'd guess a fair percentage of those were not measuring WIP.

## CLIENT SATISFACTION

If your client is happy with the service or product you provide, there is a fair chance they will recommend you to others. This is how organic growth works (see Skill 28). When a happy client moves to a new organisation, they take you with them. Over the years this means slow steady growth, with loyal clients.

But the reverse is also true. Lose a client here and there and soon you are letting staff go, due to lack of work. Too many unhappy clients, and you'll be out of business. You need to measure repeat clients, and take action immediately to win them back if they go elsewhere.

The target should be:

> ➤ Repeat work from every client.

I can't stress enough how important this is. Set your business up so either you or someone else has the time to measure these areas. If you have a bookkeeper and an online accounting system, nearly all this information, apart from WIP, will be generated for you. You just need to make a routine, and look at it.

Friday morning, Thursday afternoon, it matters not. But please just do it.

# SKILL 26

## THE BUSINESS OWNER'S PERSPECTIVE

It took me a while to realise this. The way I experienced the working day as the boss, was very different from how staff experienced it. I'll give you an example to explain what I mean.

Let's assume you drive home one evening and pull up on your drive. You look around and notice the neighbours have a different car on their drive, and there's some rubbish bags in their front garden. Your grass needs cutting. You walk in your front door, have a look round to check everything's ok, and you notice your kitchen worktops are messy from breakfast. Your husband greets you, and you sense he's a little stressed. Concerned, you ask him about his day and listen lovingly.

You take everything in, because you have an interest in your home and the people in it.

The next morning you drive to work, pull into the car park. There's a new oil patch in one of the bays, but you are oblivious to it, and to the car in one of your parking spaces. You enter the office not noticing the black bin liners in the hall, then into the toilet, completely ignoring the two empty toilet rolls on the sink.

You enter the office smiling saying hello while settling at your desk.

You take hardly anything in, because unlike your home, you have no interest in this place, you hardly give it a second thought.

The poor boss experiences things very differently. He or she has interest in both places. Trust me, it's hell sometimes, the boss sees everything.

I remember driving to work consumed with thoughts about issues at work. If I happened to be in a bad mood, I'd have to leave that in the car park – the boss must always enter the office with a cheery disposition; his or her mood sets the tone for the office.

The boss would definitely notice the oil patch, which lowers the tone of the car park, and who the hell has parked in one of her parking spaces? The black bin liners in the hall drives her mad and she just has to move them. Entering the toilet and seeing the empty toilet rolls is just too much and prompts a call to the cleaner.

Entering the office is a minefield. First scanning every staff member for anything that stands out, like a face with a hangover, or a mood. Then on to say good morning to every person, passing on pleasantries and making sure they are doing what they are supposed to be doing. Then after twenty minutes of attending to everyone else, finally you get to sit at your desk and take a deep breath. The rest of the day is much the same.

In short, the boss has an interest in the office and the team, and like the parent at home, she is receptive to everything.

So please, don't ever think that as the boss you can just turn up for work on autopilot.

## DEALING WITH REQUESTS

One thing I wasn't really prepared for as the boss, was the constant requests for various things from staff. Things like, can I have next Wednesday off, can I have three days off next week to study for my exam, could I have an advance on my wage, can I have a pay rise, can I have a car... the list goes on.

This is a tough one. On the one hand, you don't want to upset the staff member, but on the other, it could be inconvenient, and it could also cost you. It could also be seen as favouring that staff member, upsetting others. So how do you make the decision?

To be honest, I have no formula. It depends on your sense of fairness, where you draw the line. I think we all have a sense when someone is taking advantage, so when that point is reached, I usually draw the line.

If you get it wrong, the worst case is you lose a staff member, and you may bend a little if you think there is a likelihood of that happening. However, there is an opportunity in every situation. Let's say you actually want to get rid of the employee. This would be a good time to refuse the request.

In truth, I've become a lot better at dealing with requests such as these over the years, as I have developed a feel, based on a firm sense of fairness, which usually stands me in good stead.

## COUNSELLOR

You'd do well to read up on counselling skills, because I've found my life at work has been more counsellor than boss. Catering for the needs of each and every person in the office, listening to worries, helping where you can and doing your best to support and develop. It's quite draining.

But don't expect that kind of attention back, because in my experience it won't happen. I think there's only been one person, apart from my sons, who's ever asked me how I'm feeling, and if everything's ok. It's just not in their mind to do so. They assume the boss is self-sufficient and emotionally bullet proof. Which I have become over the years.

This, then, my aspiring entrepreneurs, is the life of the boss. You spend your day acting like a superhero. You must never have a mood, remain consistent at all times, never get too excited or too down. You must be there for the team at all times, always look up when they enter your office, attend to their needs, stroke them, treat them and laugh at their jokes, never expect anything in return. Then, and only then, will you get around five hours' work out of them. Ok I exaggerate, five and a half!

# PART 4:
## GROWING YOUR BUSINESS

# SKILL 27

## NEEDS, WANTS, COMMODITIES, USPs AND NICHES

This is an exciting time in any business owner's career. You've got through the first couple of years and you feel confident enough to grow the business.

I grew my business to varying degrees in the early days, only to be right back where I started a couple of years later. Then I learned the concepts I'm going to share with you here, which helped me understand how to grow the business steadily and sustainably.

First the concept is that of 'needs' and 'wants'.

### NEEDS

'Need' products are those that humans require for life, such as food, water, clothing and shelter, and also products that we have become accustomed to having and are plentiful, such as electricity, petrol, and so on. Many services are in this category, such as building and repair services, and many of the professions.

If you sell a 'need' product, your aim is to make it a 'want'. If you sell a 'want' product, your aim is to make it a 'need'. Let me explain.

Let's assume you sell bottled water. There are probably tens of brands of water, so how does the consumer decide which one to buy? With so many available all similar quality, you'd probably buy the cheapest.

Therefore, if you sell water, your aim is to make people 'want' to buy your water. This is the challenge: how do you make people prefer to buy your product?

Companies try all sorts of marketing tricks, water in different shaped bottles, with flavourings, smart water, mineral water, sparkling water, water from natural sources, all designed to get you to 'want' their water.

## WANTS

People never need 'wants', but they desire them. A 'want' is an emotion purchase rather than logic, as salespeople know only too well. How many of us have been tempted to pay more than we wanted for a new car, because the salesperson put the limited edition in front of us?

A Ferrari is an extreme example of a 'want'. I actually need a Ferrari, well that's what I tell the other half. But seriously, we don't buy a £250,000 car because we need it. A Ferrari is an emotional purchase, as is a Gucci handbag or Rolex, and marketers know this only too well, designing campaigns aimed directly at our emotions. Hence the sexy lady on the bonnet.

If you sell 'want' products, your challenge is to make them 'needs'. Take chocolate for example. We don't 'need' it, well, some of us may do, but we do like it and want it sometimes. So the job of a company selling chocolate is to find ways through marketing and taste to make you 'want' their chocolate over other brands. In fact, although they'd rarely admit it, to make you addicted to their chocolate. Cigarettes are a case in point.

Have a think about your product or service. It should be fairly easy for you to work out if it's a 'need' or a 'want'. Now work out how you can make your 'need' a 'want' and vice versa.

## COMMODITIES

Many products that serve people's everyday needs have become plentiful. Many do not vary greatly from supplier to supplier. The only difference is the way they are marketed. There's a lot of competition in the commodity market, which can drive down prices and make it an uncomfortable place to trade.

The construction sector, for example, has been commoditised, in that there are thousands of construction companies able to provide a similar quality and service. The only difference is price. If you were having an extension built, would you pay £50k when you could get it for £40k?

In construction, you are only able to charge as much as the lowest price someone is willing to do it for; your price is capped to that level.

Some luxury 'want' products start out life as unique or special, like the mobile phone, with high price tags. But over time as other companies copy the original, they become more available and competition reduces the price, until the product becomes commoditised, like mobile phones have today.

Do you sell a commodity? If so, how can you get an edge in the market?

## UNIQUE SELLING PROPOSITIONS (USP)

If you sell a commodity product, what can you do to increase price or sell more? It's difficult, because by definition, a commodity is not unique. But there are things you can do. Take our construction company, for example. As a construction company, we understand we are a commodity; in other words, we mostly fulfil a need; we also understand that there are many competitors that can fulfil the same need. So our aim is to make people 'want' to use our services.

In our business, we achieve this by working out what is important to our clients and what we could do that would make them choose us over a competitor. We call these the clients' 'hot buttons'. Then, once we understand their requirement, we adapt our service to meet their hot buttons.

Understanding what is important to our clients enables us to develop our USPs.

Hot buttons will be different for every client, so the skill is adapting your service to meet differing needs. That means great flexibility and communication within your business.

## NICHING

Another way of gaining an edge in a commodity market is to niche. Niching is to limit your service to a small section of the market.

For example, in our business we limit our service to Healthcare, Leisure, Blue Light and Education; we are expert in these fields. We understand our client's hot buttons and we are very experienced in this type of work. For example, there are not many companies that have the expertise to work next to a live operating theatre and cause no disruption. This makes us attractive to hospitals.

This strategy allows us to approach clients in these sectors and offer services specifically designed to meet their needs, and we advertise that fact.

We also limit the size of project we take on. This allows us to hone our systems, processes and staff training, specifically for those types of projects and this makes us very efficient and able to keep overheads low.

In this kind of commoditised market, it is very difficult to de-commoditise, but now you understand how you can at least minimise competition.

# SKILL 28

## ORGANIC AND DRIVEN GROWTH

I've learned that there are two main ways to grow your business, apart from merging with or buying another business. The first is organic growth, the second my son calls driven growth, as in, driving sales into the business. Both require very different approaches.

### ORGANIC GROWTH

Organic growth refers to growth by repeat work and referrals. Observe the tree below. It represents the potential for growth in your company.

The branches represent clients. The trunk represents your first client. Do good work for your fist client and they'll introduce you to their colleague. Client one could change job, and offer you work with his new organisation. Meantime, you are still doing great work for client two. He introduces you to his colleagues, clients three and four. Your client base and turnover are growing steadily, and there is no reason why this situation shouldn't carry on forever, so long as you remember one thing. A tree needs sun and rain to thrive. A business needs to maintain high levels of service and quality.

In my experience, this is where companies go wrong – they either begin to take clients for granted, or spread themselves too thin, and service drops. Service levels and quality must be maintained at all costs, or limbs of your tree will be lopped off, and you'll never know how much work you will have lost in the future.

If you cut off too many limbs, the tree dies.

The rule of organic growth is very clear:

> Maintain quality and service.

Organic growth is absolutely essential and it could sustain your business for ever, so long as you keep up service and quality.

One point on organic growth to be aware of. Sometimes, for no fault of your own, a client stops giving you work. This could be due to relocation, changing job, getting sacked or just retiring. Therefore, you are leaving a lot to chance if your strategy is based solely on organic growth. Better to consider a joint strategy of organic and driven growth, thus replacing any clients you lose, and adding in new ones.

## DRIVEN GROWTH

Driven growth is actively bringing in sales, through sales and marketing strategies, and I would strongly recommend you consider a sales and marketing strategy from day one.

## SALES AND MARKETING

Sales and marketing has become a generic term, but in my experience, sales and marketing are two completely different approaches to driving revenue into a business.

Sales can be very specific. Sales or the salesperson has two functions: sell more to existing clients, and target new clients, prospects as they are called.

Marketing is more general, aimed at raising your company profile and generating new leads.

In a start-up or small company, overheads may dictate that the same person does the sales and marketing, as I did for many years, but I've found the two require different personality types. While the salesperson will be customer facing and usually extrovert, preferring to be out of the office, marketing these days is mainly office based, so a creative nature is preferred.

## SALES

A salesperson's primary function is to increase sales in your business. To make approaches to prospects who may have a need for your product or service. To build relationships with buyers in those companies and constantly look for opportunities to sell to new and existing clients.

I've employed many salespeople, and I've found them among the most challenging to manage. I've had a few that think their job is driving around all day having cups of tea with people, or sitting in the office on the phone all day. It's not; a salesperson should be in front of prospects most of their time.

Unlike office based employees, you have no way of knowing where your salespeople are. There are customer relationship management systems (CRMs) which can manage your sales team's movements, but I've found these don't work. Prospects often change meetings at short notice, or want to meet in the evening, so your salesperson needs autonomy, and should be very flexible and driven.

I've learned to only ever employ salespeople on commission, with a small basic pay, and to set them clear sales targets. This provides incentive to sell and enables your salesperson to manage their own time.

One more tip: make the targets very simple. Number of new prospect visits per week for example. Or revenue brought in per quarter. You don't need a long sales report, just the number of visits that week.

## MARKETING

Marketing is not so easy to define. This is because it is unique to every company, and is only limited by the marketer's creativity.

The essence of marketing is to drive in growth by making people aware of and wanting what you have to offer. To get that in front of consumers in any way they can, and as many times as they can. There are many ways you can achieve this, which are beyond the scope of this book or my experience.

There is an amazing website by Splash Copywriters (www. splashcopywriters.com) who discuss one-hundred and fifty-nine examples of marketing. A great place to start for marketing ideas.

## PRIORITIES

There is one more point I must add here for all existing and prospective business owners.

You should be absolutely clear that your primary responsibility is bringing in work. You should allocate most of your time to this. Delegate to your sales team by all means, but if work dries up, there's only one person to blame.

Please do not detract from this, keep your energy focussed where it needs to be, even when times are good.

# SKILL 29

## SERVICE VS PROFIT

One of my biggest values as a young managing director was a natural desire for quality and service, never money. I reasoned that if I focused on great service, I'd be successful, and the money would follow, and it did.

More than thirty years in business, and I still stand by that. I've never been money focussed but I've always been obsessed about the quality of service we provide. Especially as we operate in a commodity market, as I've explained in Skill 27.

The business thrived in those early years with that philosophy, and we did indeed make a lot of money. Then around ten years into the business, following a lean couple of years, I strayed from my core values and tended to let profit become our main driver, announcing this half-heartedly to the team.

It backfired on me big time. I found that service dropped as the team prioritised profit. We were not as flexible with clients, trying to squeeze every penny out of the contract, and we lost a lot of repeat work.

Reality kicked in around a year later, after we had one of our worst years ever. I had to eat humble pie and go back to the team and tell them I was wrong.

Prioritising money didn't feel right anyway, it's not who I am, and my strong belief is that anyone who prioritises money over service in any business is bound to fail.

If you focus on money, that's what you spend most of your energy thinking about, and not where it should be, on improving service and making people want to use you.

If you can solve a problem for your clients, or give them something that makes their lives easier or better, make them look good in the eyes of their boss and make the experience enjoyable and reliable... Then money will follow.

# SKILL 30

## FINANCING GROWTH

Growing a business costs money, it's an investment, and there's no certainty the investment will pay off. This is what makes entrepreneurs different from most people – they are willing to risk money for their dream.

Generally speaking, there are only two ways to get money to invest in growth. Money from your reserves, or from outside sources.

## RESERVES

I realised early on that I wanted to build a meaningful business that I could pass on to my children, which I have now done. Now it's looking like the business will be passed to their children.

I've only been able to achieve this because I've left a large part of the profits in the business year on year. These are called cash reserves.

This not only makes my balance sheet (Skill 36) look good to outside investors and the bank, it has given me funds to invest back into the business for growth.

I believe having cash reserves in your business is absolutely essential. Businesses, like everything else in life, follow the inevitable cycle of peaks and troughs. Having reserves enables you to weather the storms. Many businesses go under because the owners take all the profits to minimise corporation tax, and when the inevitable downturn comes, or they need money to grow, they have no cash available.

One note on this. I've been advised by some accountants to take dividends or buy things like plant and even cars to reduce profit at the year-end. I feel this is bad advice. I've found that some accountants have a short-term view of business, looking at the figures today, rather than from a strategic long-term perspective. I've seen inexperienced business owners driving new cars and buying big houses, when the business is only a few years old. What they should be doing is investing back into their business, waiting until they are established before they get caught up with shiny toys. You must be strong if you get this sort of advice. Put some cash away for a rainy day and pay the tax.

My formula for the amount of cash reserves you should hold, is around three-four percent of turnover. If your sales are ten million, you should have between three and four hundred thousand in the savings account. I've found this to be enough for investment and to weather the occasional storm.

## BANKS

It's well worth building a good relationship with two banks as discussed in Skill 15. If it goes wrong with one, you have a track-record with the other. Another tip is to have your personal account with the same bank as your primary business account. It makes it easier for their verification process and money transfers, and it provides more comfort to the bank.

Banks do get a bad rap, but to be fair, they have helped me out on more than one occasion. Barclays agreed a loan for me in twenty-four hours once, to help me buy a property.

There's a lot of bureaucracy with banks, which is why it's worth sticking with the same ones. But once you understand their priorities, they are easier to deal with. In short, banks want to know how they are going to get their money back. End of. They will make sure their loan is protected and double protected. They will certainly want security, and they will almost certainly want you to give a debenture (priority payment in an insolvency) or personal guarantee. Which overrides the protection of the limited company, and makes you personally liable.

My relationship manager, as they are now called, once told me that banks lend to people not businesses. I don't know if that is true, but I do know that I have found it easier to obtain loans because I have built up a good level of trust with the bank over many years.

One tip I must pass on, is to keep close to your manager. Call him or her at least once a month for a chat. Get to know them, tell them how you're doing. Let them know what's coming up, and what's going on at the firm. Banks want to know two things before they will trust you:

> ➢ You understand the finances.
> ➢ You are in control of the finances.

Prove this by letting them know you are in control, and you know what's going on with the finances. Speak their language, drop in the terminology, P&L, gross margin, net margin, overheads, cash flow and show them the spreadsheets to back it up.

If you master this, the chances of your manager arguing your case to their boss if you need a loan will vastly increase.

My manager Richard is a good guy, I met him recently in McDonald's. It's a small price to pay for the many loans I've had from him over the years.

One more thing. Never be afraid to change your bank or manager as I have. Once when a manager wanted a personal security from me, which I felt was unfair, and once when a young manager wanted to see monthly cash-flow statements I wasn't prepared to provide. Our finances were great at the time, so I notified my old manager, and they had him replaced.

## OTHER INVESTMENT

There are many other ways to find outside money to help grow your business. In some cases, this involves handing over equity (shares) in your business, something I'd never do. Giving equity means losing some control; however, in certain circumstances it may be the only way to raise capital.

Here are some other ways to raise capital. I am not an expert in any of these, but as a business owner you need to be aware they exist. The main ones to consider are:

## ANGEL INVESTORS

Angels can be anyone, from family members to someone you meet at the golf club. They are usually affluent people who could be time poor and cash rich. Angel investing is more prominent nowadays with interest rates being so low for so long, and bank returns being so minimal.

## CROWD FUNDING

Still a relatively new form of raising finance, crowd funding works by lots of investors offering small amounts of money to support a new venture. Risk is limited across the pool of investors and crowd funding is becoming a popular method of raising finance for business start-ups.

Crowd funding has been criticised for the lack of regulation, but crowd funders have recently formed the UK Crowdfunding Association, which is a step in the right direction. The Financial Services Association (FCA) advise investors to proceed with caution.

## VENTURE CAPITALISTS (VC)

This is an established way of raising finance for start-ups, businesses in their early stages and research and development. Venture capitalists are typically high wealth individuals or groups of investors, experienced business people in their own right. They look for companies they feel have high growth potential.

VCs are expensive. They look for high returns, in the region of 20% to 30% or more annually. They typically require equity in the business too, sometimes a majority holding.

## PENSION FUNDS

A pension fund is another good way to fund your business, particularly to purchase plant or property, but only commercial property. I've had a Small Self-Administered Pension Scheme (SSAS) for many years, and have bought several commercial properties through the fund, from which the company has traded, and another for investment purposes. Pension funds will not consider residential property at all.

The rent owed to the fund is paid directly into your pension, and is tax free. It's a very useful way of buying commercial property, topping up your pension with the rent, and also of reducing profit.

The pension fund can also lend 50% of the total amount held in the fund, back to your business as working capital, so long as it is fully secured on a first charge. This is expensive, the interest rate is high, and at the time of writing the maximum loan period is five years. Also, the loan is paid back on a capital and interest basis. Of course, all the payments are straight into your pension.

Loans can also be used to pay off other higher interest loans or for working capital. They are also a great way of reducing profit by tax free contribution to the fund.

I would strongly advise you to look into an SSAS and contact a pension actuary for further information, as they can be very useful for smaller businesses.

Pension funds are governed by very strict government lending criteria, and you should use a good actuary for advice. I use a company based in London called Nigel Sloam & Co, and have found them to be very helpful indeed.

Another important point regarding SSASs, is that they can be very useful from an inheritance perspective, as they can easily be passed down the generations, tax free. Unfortunately, the government have capped the total allowance per person at £1m, at the time of writing.

# SKILL 31

## WHAT IS MY EXIT ROUTE?

**You may be wondering why I've included a section on exiting your business under the 'growing your business' section. Let me explain.**

Many people believe you should plan your exit right at the outset, when you are planning your business, and with good reason.

Let's assume you know from day one that you only want the business for ten years, then you'll sell. That decision will affect many things about how you set up and run the business.

For example, the type of people you employ. You'll be on the lookout for individuals with the right aptitude, who may want to run their own business one day, someone you could perhaps mentor into the role.

This would also affect the role you play in the business. When the time came to sell, if you were still a key person in the business, you'd struggle to sell. Businesses where the owner manager is key, rarely sell for much, as the goodwill (client relationships) tend to leave along with the owner.

It could also affect the amount and number of assets you build up in the business, and cash reserves you hold.

In my first business, I planned to have management buy the company from me. Things changed as my sons left school and joined the business, all five of them. I went from sole proprietor, to family business, and my exit route changed drastically. There was no way the boys were going to let me sell the company they had invested the early years of their lives in.

When we got to a point that we knew some of the sons were interested in continuing with the business, we started talking about a succession plan. Succession from one generation to the next needs very careful planning; it can be a very difficult and emotional process indeed. Putting deep thought into how we were going to achieve this many years before, was very useful, and enabled us to write the succession plan.

It took five years in-all for my second son Ben to succeed me as MD, at the age of twenty-eight. The same age I had become MD.

The fact that my sons were taking over the business meant my exit strategy changed drastically. We invested heavily in the boys' development, and began to buy long-term appreciating assets such as property.

One of the downsides of bringing your children through to the senior positions in your business, is the effect this has on other senior staff. I lost two senior managers and good friends over this, as they felt the writing was on the wall for their progression in the business. Something that was, in fact, true.

So, you can begin to understand that looking very long-term at your exit will affect many areas of your business strategy today.

You'll be wise to plan for this as early as you can, and adapt your plans if things change.

Here are some common exit routes. Again, I'm not expert in most of these apart from handing on to family members, but as an entrepreneur you need to at least have awareness of them all.

> Hand the company to a family member or members. This is a tricky and emotional process.
> A management buy-out (MBO) where the business is sold to one or more key employees, usually over an agreed period of time.
> Sell to other shareholders.
> Sell to another party, perhaps a competitor.
> If the company is large, enter into an Initial Public Offering (IPO).
> You could employ a management team and retain ownership for a wage and dividend.
> You could liquidate the company.

One more very important lesson I learned regarding exit routes is tax. Get tax advice very early on, day one in fact. The decisions you make at the beginning could come back and bite you with a tax bill if you don't involve a good tax accountant early in the process.

You have been warned.

175

# PART 5:
## MUST KNOW FINANCIALS

Have you ever seen Dragons' Den? Firstly, you shouldn't be watching telly, you should be developing yourself, reading or listening to educational videos. But as it's Dragons' Den, I'll forgive you.

Theo Paphitis asks the entrepreneur, "What's your expected turnover, gross and net profit for the coming year?"

The entrepreneur stands there sweating, looking blank and twitching, and eventually mumbles some figures. He clearly hasn't a clue what Theo is talking about. You do not want to be that person, for two reasons. One, you'll look like a plonker, and two, you'll survive about ten minutes in business.

One contradictory note on this. After he had already made millions, Richard Branson famously owned-up to not understanding the difference between gross and net profit. There's an exception to every rule.

As an entrepreneur, it's not essential to understand accounts like an accountant, but I have found it essential to have a good level of knowledge to enable me to understand financial language and to safeguard my business.

The good thing about double entry bookkeeping and our accounting system in general, is that it is a universal concept, used in all countries, with few small exceptions.

I'm going to go through the parts you must know here, and these are applicable to any type of business.

But before I get into the numbers, to give you a more rounded view, I will talk to you about the accounts people. The right accounts people are absolutely vital to your early success. I've found them to be a tricky bunch to work with, and I'll share with you my experience of recruiting and working with the bookkeeper, management accountant and chartered accountant.

# SKILL 32

## THE ACCOUNTS PEOPLE

Before we get into the financials, it's definitely worth taking a moment to talk to you about the people involved in your accounts team. What to expect from them and how to deal with them. Starting with your bookkeeper.

### BOOKKEEPER

The bookkeeper is an overhead, but one of your most valuable assets. Why? Because if you are in the dark with your figures, you could go under without even knowing, and thousands of businesses do. Being in the dark is dangerous and very stressful. If you want to build a meaningful business, you must know your figures, daily, weekly, monthly and yearly. But I digress.

I've worked with maybe ten bookkeepers in my career, and trust me when I say, there are some poor ones out there, and it's very difficult to tell at interview whether you have a good one or not, as they all speak the accounts lingo. My advice is, put them on as long a probation period as possible, at least six months. A bad bookkeeper can do major damage to your company. Not least get you in trouble with the Inland Revenue if they file inadequate figures, which has happened to us recently.

Your bookkeeper must have a certain personality type. Firstly, they must be able to sit in an office all day working on figures. Not everyone's cup of tea, and they must be analytical and detailed, the type that drives me mad, being a big picture person.

I've found them to be very territorial – they have files for everything, which are always placed in exactly the same place, and even the boss dares not move them.

They are generally not extroverts. I used to get irritated that my bookkeeper sat in her chair all day rarely communicating with anyone. Then my management accountant John pointed out, did I want the office butterfly managing my books, or did I want someone who was capable of sitting all day and producing methodical figures? I got the point.

It is possible to outsource your bookkeeping, but as you grow, your bookkeeper should be among your first member of staff. Why? Because as I have said, you must always know your figures, and you'll not get up-to-date figures quickly enough by outsourcing to an accountant.

In small companies, the bookkeeper is usually the one chasing your debts, and I have found this to be an issue on occasions. Credit control is best carried out over the phone, and bookkeepers in my experience are generally not telephone people. So your credit control (chasing money and cash flow, Skill 37) suffers. Try to separate out the credit control from the accounts as soon as you can.

I did have one bookkeeper, Joyce, many years ago, who was capable in all areas. I inherited her from my dad, a wonderful lady and a meticulous bookkeeper. She was with me nearly seventeen years until she retired.

Trust is a big issue with bookkeepers. In Skill 15, I mentioned a bookkeeper who stole £24,000 from my company over a four-year period. I naively and stupidly gave her the same trust I had given Joyce, and from week two she paid herself overtime she never did. Small but regular amounts, and a few big amounts.

We dismissed her with garden leave, writing off the money. Then out of the blue, she took us to an industrial tribunal for wrongful dismissal, which we of course won.

I tell you this story to make you aware that this sort of thing happens. You, or someone you trust, must sign off everything of a financial nature, especially the payroll. Again, you have been warned.

There is an unwritten code with bookkeepers, their loyalty lies only with the boss. They do not, under any circumstances, discuss figures with anyone, unless explicitly instructed to do so by you. As you grow and employ a financial director (FD), this may change. If you find out they have broken this trust, let them go immediately.

There's one more story I'd like to tell about an unsavoury trait one of my bookkeepers had, the same one that stole £24,000 from us. I remember she question me one day, when I asked her to transfer money to my personal account. She questioned the fact that I was paying myself money and not the staff. I was shocked. I soon realised she was an envious, resentful person.

Make sure your bookkeeper doesn't show signs of envy. This lady looked for opportunities to make snide comments about money. She was all for the workers, and against the management. You cannot work with a bookkeeper with that attitude. They know more about your finances than you do, every penny you take and give. They must be a trusted confidant to you, and bear no resentment whatever you decide to do with the money. Many businesses I know employ family members in this position, until they are of a certain size, and I can understand why.

In conclusion, please be very careful when you recruit your bookkeeper, and always put them on a six-month probation so you have plenty of time to uncover any poor personality traits or lack of skill.

## MANAGEMENT ACCOUNTANT

Where the bookkeeper is all about day-to-day keeping of accurate accounts, the management accountant is about strategy. He or she uses the up-to-date financial data produced by the bookkeeper, and makes the necessary checks and adjustments such as work in progress (Skill 40) to build an accurate picture of where the business is at, financially.

The purpose of producing management accounts is twofold. Firstly, to highlight any poor performing areas of the business, and also for management to plan future strategy. They are absolutely vital to safeguard your business and give you an early warning of any problems, so you have time to address them before it's too late.

I strongly advise you to engage a management accountant to produce monthly accounts, including a profit and loss, balance sheet, cash flow and work in progress, all discussed in the coming sections. This can be carried out in one to two days per month, depending on the size of the company, so it will not cost a fortune.

The management accountant is usually a different personality type to the accountant and bookkeeper, and I do generalise. They have the analytical side, but also the creative side which enables them to use the figures to drive performance. It can be exciting sitting with a management accountant, watching them interpret the figures and suggesting ways to improve the business.

In the early stages, you may need to outsource your management accounts. They will take one-to-two days a month to produce, and much of this can be done off site with a networked accounts system.

I have had the privilege to work with a great management accountant, John Trueman, for many years; he is mainly responsible for my knowledge today. John's motto is as follows. Turnover is vanity, profit is sanity, cash is reality. A good one to remember, when all around you are telling you to spend or grow turnover.

## CHARTERED ACCOUNTANT

At the time of writing, if your turnover in the UK is more than £10.2m, it's a requirement to have audited accounts. This means you must have a chartered or certified accountant audit your financial systems.

The audit itself is a time consuming, invasive event that can take several days. Your accountant will send in an accounts clerk who will go through your computer and paper files with a fine-toothed comb to make sure they are compliant, and it won't be cheap.

Accountants these days have a lot of regulation imposed on them from the Inland Revenue and their own professional body, and this can sometimes make it feel like they are working for the government, and not you.

If you are under the threshold for audit and just need year-end accounts, you could choose not to engage a qualified accountant, and use a good management accountant – it will probably cost you less than half the price.

Accountants come into their own when advising on matters outside of annual accounting, such as new ventures, tax issues, corporate structuring, property purchases and long-term financial planning. If it's your intention to engage in any of these activities any time in the future, you have no choice but to pay the fee and get advice from an accountant. When I say you have no choice, I mean, if you don't get the advice, it could cost you a lot more than the fee in the long run. For example, if you were considering buying property in the business, there could be very tax efficient ways you may not be aware of. A few hours of an accountant's time could save you a small fortune down the line.

However, it is true to say that whenever I see an accountancy fee, it usually makes me wince.

Another good pointer when working with your accountant is to get advice very early on in the thinking stage, especially about tax implications. That way you can factor the advice into your thinking for an even better outcome.

## ENGAGING AN ACCOUNTANT.

I've interviewed many accountants, and there's been a common theme to their sales pitch. The usual line is that they will save you their fees in tax. They never have in my case. In my experience, the government have closed up all the loopholes for smaller businesses, so there's not much they can do to save tax.

I've also noticed some accountants have far too many clients, and they will never disclose this at interview. I've found this leads to poor service, and a feeling of being a number rather than a valued client. But this has only been my experience.

All in all, an accountant is a must in business. If you are going to do deals other than normal trading, my advice is to pay for a good one, a few thousand a year more could save you a few hundred thousand on a big deal. Even if at the time, the fee seems unreasonably high.

One more thing, make sure you like the person. You must feel a connection. He or she will know more about the finances of the businesses than you do, so you must feel comfortable in their company and able to discuss fees for example, openly.

# SKILL 33

## TURNOVER - GROSS PROFIT - NET PROFIT

These are the essentials. I'll explain what they mean here, and explain how they are used to manage your business in Skill 42: Preparing your annual budget.

### TURNOVER

Sometimes called revenue or sales. This is the total amount of goods or services invoiced in a particular period, the total sales for the period, which could be a month, quarter or full year, known as financial year. You can have your financial year end date, any month you wish, the last day of that month. That's turnover, as easy as that.

### GROSS PROFIT

To explain the concept, let's assume you did a job and invoiced the client £100. You bought £20 worth of materials and it cost you £60 in labour. These are the total 'direct costs', £80. Otherwise known as cost of sale. The gross profit is what is left over, £20. Usually expressed as a percentage 20%.

This is set out in a standard profit and loss (P&L) format below:

Sale          £100
Materials     £20
Labour        £60
Gross profit  £20

It works exactly the same with the whole year's turnover. For example, £10m in sales, £8m in direct costs, giving a gross profit of £2m or 20%.

I wish I could say that 20% was all yours, but there's a little something called overheads that need paying first. These are the running costs of the business, discussed in detail in the next skill.

## NET PROFIT

This is the good bit that's left over for you, after you've paid tax that is. In the above example the gross profit is £20.

However, you still have general bills, such as utilities, rent or mortgage, stationery, vehicles, fuel, and general running costs. These collectively are known as overheads. Some staff costs are sometimes also put into overheads, such as directors and administration staff, where they cannot easily be apportioned to any particular job.

Accounts terminology speaks of 'contribution'. That is how much profit a particular project has contribution to the monthly overhead. In our example, the contribution to monthly overheads is £20.

# SKILL 34

## OVERHEADS

Overheads have their own section because you need to understand what they are and how they can cause you major problems if you don't keep them under control.

Overheads are any costs that cannot directly be attributed to the project. They are all the other stuff you need, or sometimes don't need but want, to run your business, including:

➢ Utilities
➢ Motor vehicles
➢ Petrol
➢ Stationery
➢ IT equipment
➢ Office furniture
➢ Office maintenance
➢ Directors and administrative staff salaries (this varies company to company)
➢ Training
➢ Phones
➢ Subscriptions
➢ Accountancy fees
➢ Etc...

This will vary greatly depending on which sector your company operates in and from company to company, but you get the picture.

## OVERHEADS HAVE LEGS

The late Felix Dennis said in his book, How to Get Rich, "overheads have legs and they can run away with you". How true that is.

I found in my early days in business, overheads used to increase when I had spare money in the bank, burning a hole in my pocket. I remember being tempted to buy stuff, just because I had spare cash, not because the business really needed it. A little luxury here, a little there, it seemed harmless enough. But when the quarterly accounts came in, and I saw the consequences of all that spending I soon learned to spend only if absolutely essential to the business.

That said, if you must treat yourself from spare cash, pay for it now, don't take on long-term debt, such as new vehicle finance or monthly software agreements. A quick hit that you can afford is one thing, but long-term additional overhead is another. We once bought a fleet of Mercedes when we were flush in the bank, but it didn't last long, and when times became hard again, they all went back.

As Felix Dennis said, overheads can get out of control very easily; that is my experience too. Take for example the humble office pen. In our near paperless world, it always amazes me how on almost all quarterly stationery orders, there was a box of fifty Bic pens. That means we lose more than a pen every other day, the whole year.

Another more expensive example is vehicles and petrol.

I've worked with directors who absolutely positively must have a fleet of vehicles. Why? Again, this is inexperience and short-sightedness. Remember, after a peak always comes a trough. Load-up on vehicles and other overheads in a peak at your peril. You'll be arguing with the finance company to return the vehicles as we did, in the trough. I hate to say this, but you've been told, again.

Company cars also breed misuse of benefit. For example, during an audit many years ago, we found an employee who was mainly office based, had receipts on two consecutive days for a full tank of petrol. He later owned up to filling his wife's car up.

Mobile phone bills are another good example. Sometimes our mobile data bill is astonishing. People make international phone calls, because they are not footing the bill.

So, that said, let's take a look at the following example to see how overheads fit in to the profit and loss statement:

| Sales | £100 |
|---|---|
| Materials | £20 |
| Labour | £60 |
| Gross profit | £20 |
| Overheads | £14 or 14% |
| Net profit before tax | £6 or 6% |

Out of £100, you get £6, less corporation tax at 19% at the time of writing, and then of course personal tax which probably leaves you with around £3 if you are lucky.

You can easily see that if overheads do get out of control, your 14% can soon become 18%, and your net profit reduces to 2%. Or worse, 14% becomes 21%, and you've made a loss.

I didn't say it was easy to make money.

My advice is to have your bookkeeper provide an itemised list of overheads monthly. These will be produced for you on your profit and loss statement on your computerised accounting system. You, or your financial director, must check these regularly.

My advice is, clamp down on overheads, keep them under control – you'll not be popular, but you will remain in business.

# SKILL 35

## PROFIT AND LOSS

The financial summary of a trading period – usually a year

Profit and Loss, known to the accounting profession and the entrepreneur as P&L.

Your P&L is as important to you as a navigation system to an aeroplane. Without it you are flying in the dark. Not having a P&L to hand 24/7 is a grave mistake and has been the ruin of many a business.

Your computerised accounting software will have an up to the minute P&L, and although it does not account for work in progress or adjustments, this is a very useful financial guide.

At the end of the financial year, your P&L will form the basis of your financial report for that period. It will show your turnover, cost of sale, gross profit, itemised overheads and net profit. It will look something like this:

## PROFIT & LOSS STATEMENT

| | |
|---|---|
| Turnover (sales) | £100 |
| Cost of Sale (purchases) | |
| Materials | £20 |
| Labour | £60 |
| Gross profit | £20 |
| Overheads (itemized) | £14 |
| Net profit before tax | £6 |

Most reasonable sized companies will have overheads of more than a page long and itemised cost of sales probably half that. I've prepared some more detailed P&Ls for you at my book website at *www.carmelcresttraining.com/50skills*

# SKILL 36

## BALANCE SHEET

The financial summary of your trading history, from day one.

The balance sheet represents your entire trading history from day one. It shows the position of the company overall, including all the money you have saved, property owned, other assets and liabilities.

The P&L is only interested in your financial performance; the balance sheet takes account of several other issues, such as:

- ➢ Fixed Assets
- ➢ Current Assets
- ➢ Current Liabilities
- ➢ Long-term Liabilities
- ➢ Capital and Reserves

I'll explain these one by one.


### FIXED ASSETS

Hopefully you've reinvested some of your previous profits as I advised. Maybe you have bought property, plant, machinery or vehicles. These are known as your fixed assets. Some appreciate, such as property; some depreciate, such as plant.

Fixed assets are what give you meat on the bone, as I call it, or strength in depth, and banks love to see this. It means you are serious about business.

Think of it like this: squirrels hide away nuts in the summer, when they are plentiful – they know that winter is just around the corner. In your business, you'd be wise to invest some of your profits into reserves, in property or appreciating assets, to get you through the bad winters, and there will be bad winters.

While fixed assets may not be able to be turned into money immediately, they show a bank, investor or a buyer you have strength in depth and you have been investing profits back in your business. You could also sell a fixed asset and turn it into working capital if you needed to. Current assets are different.

## CURRENT ASSETS

Current assets refer to assets available to you in the short-term, within a year. Usually cash in the bank or any investment that can be converted into money easily. Also, money owed to you from your clients, known as your debtors, see Skill 38.

As I keep saying, it's very important to build up cash reserves. It's a good idea to hold at least two bank accounts in your business, a current account and a savings account. When you have spare money that you are sure is excess to your cash flow requirements (see Skill 37), transfer this into a savings account you can access instantly. Preferably a high interest bank account (HIBA).

Always carry some money in reserve. I feel safe with a minimum cash reserve of 3% of turnover. For example, if turnover is £10m, then savings should be around £300k minimum.

If you manage to put some money away, life can get very interesting, even life changing. Eventually, you will accrue cash reserves of more than 3%. You could, and I believe should, invest that money into appreciating assets, such as property. This is your insurance for later in life, the beginnings of your legacy.

## CURRENT LIABILITIES

These are your short-term liabilities, the money you owe suppliers, collectively known as creditors, including any other short-term liabilities.

People often get confused with debtors and creditors. Debtors owe you money. You owe creditors money.

The simple way to remember this, is that your suppliers have extended credit to you, in that they have given you goods or services on the promise of payment. They are your creditors.

## LONG-TERM LIABILITIES

These liabilities are separated out from other liabilities because they are not immediately payable by you and could outbalance your figures, as these are owed over a long period of time.

Examples of long-term liabilities are mortgages, other loans, and pensions. Although the amount of the loan repayment owed in that year will be shown in short-term liabilities.

Long-term liabilities are separated out from short-term liabilities on the balance sheet because some clients and lenders need to know which liabilities are due within one year, and that your current assets (cash or money owed) will cover these liabilities.

## THE IMPORTANCE OF A STRONG BALANCE SHEET

If you ever go to a bank or investor to borrow money, your balance sheet is one of the first places they will look. They will go back three years or more to see the trends. This is why companies with three years or less trading history find it more difficult to obtain loans.

Lenders use what are known as financial ratios to assess your company. There are many ratios, but the most common two I use are the Current Ratio and the Working Capital Ratio.

## CURRENT RATIO

The current ratio is your current assets (cash) divided by your current liabilities (cash owed). It is a measure of your company's ability to cover its short-term debt.

For example, if your current assets were £100,000, and your current liabilities were £87,000, your score would be 1.15, which means you can cover your debts by 1.15 times. A good score is between 1 and 2.

## CAPITAL AND RESERVES

Usually at the bottom of your balance sheet will be your reserves. Reserves are cash you have decided to leave in the business at the end of the financial year. They accrue year on year. The more reserves you accrue, the stronger the business becomes.

Healthy reserves are a sign of a strong business, one that is able to weather the storm, and as I've said, this is attractive to buyers, investors and lenders.

A new entrepreneur has to be strong minded to build up reserves, and not spend the profits. If you leave profit in the business, you will pay corporation tax, and that's painful. Those who are new to business often take all the profit, often on wrongful advice from their accountant as I have said.

My advice is not to take all the profit. Take some, but leave most of it in the firm, build your reserves, build your fixed assets. You can take the money later, when your firm is in a strong financial position.

The amazing Jim Rohn tells a story about the goose that lays the golden eggs. Always feed the goose first. Don't cut bits off and kill it. A fat goose lays many golden eggs.

# SKILL 37

## CASH FLOW

In Skill 25, I spoke about the things you need to measure. This is one, if not the, most important.

What is cash flow? I explain it like this.

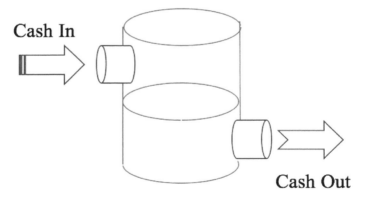

Think of your bank account as a big pot. Money from customers flows in at the top and fills it up. Money to pay suppliers, wages and overheads flows out the bottom. If it empties faster than it fills, then you have a cash flow problem. You will run out of money at some stage, and won't cover your short-term debts.

It will get to the point where the bank will not honour your payments, staff will leave, and creditors will be on the phone, or worse at the door, then file court action for their money. Your business will be in the hands of the receivers, who will sell off what they can, pay anyone with a charge on your business, usually the bank, pay themselves and other creditors, and it will be the end of your business.

The irony is that you may actually be owed enough money to cover your debts, it's just not in your bank. This is why the person who chases money, your credit controller, is so important to your business.

# SKILL 38

## CREDIT CONTROL

Most business analysts agree that poor management of money, cash flow, is the most common reason small businesses go under. I certainly agree with that.

The times when I've felt most threatened and stressed in my career, is when the company has been owed large amounts of money, and the client has held up payment. That is anxiety.

So, what can you do to prevent this from happening in your business? The general principle, as we said in Skill 37, is to speed up money coming in, and slow down money going out, and also specifically, the following life-saving list.

### GREAT CASH FLOW ESSENTIAL LIST

> ➢ Agreed payment terms up-front with customers. Don't just accept monthly, ask for weekly, fortnightly, or money up front. If you don't ask you don't get.
> ➢ Invoice the client on the day the job finishes, not at the end of the month. Established businesses with cash can invoice at the month end, but not new starters.

> Employ a great credit controller to understand the detail of each and every debt and chase it until it is in your bank.
> Try to slow down the payments going out of your business, agree longer credit terms with suppliers.

Any accounting software, such as SAGE, Quick Books etc, will have an 'aged debtor report'. This is a list of money owed to you, and when it is due. A good credit controller will live and breathe this report, and should be able to tell you how much money is expected in, and when, without referring to the report.

## LATE PAYMENT PROCESS

It is very important that you have a late payment process.

This should be activated when a payment is only one day late, and followed-up every few days thereafter, as a minimum. The process should be much more stringent for large outstanding amounts, and should include notifying a senior manager.

Unfortunately, late payment is part of business, but in my experience, the saying 'he who shouts the loudest gets heard first', is very true in credit control. No one likes confrontation, so be persistent, shout loud and shout early. It is your money!

# SKILL 39

## SALES AND PURCHASE

Sales invoices (Debtors)

You raise and send a sales invoice, a bill, to a client following the sale of goods or services.

### PURCHASE INVOICES (CREDITORS)

You receive a purchase invoice, a bill, for the work your suppliers have done for you.

That invoice from your supplier was their sales invoice. When you receive it, it becomes your purchase invoice.

This can be difficult to get your head around. To explain, I've set out the sequence of events and paperwork trail, when one company buys goods from another.

### THE PAPERWORK INVOLVED IN BUYING GOODS

> ➢ Company A needs goods, so they ask company B to quote.

➤ Company B sends quote.
➤ Company A raise a purchase order to company B, against the quote.
➤ Company B receives the order and supplies the goods.
➤ Company B sends a sales invoice for the goods to company A.
➤ Company A receives the sales invoice, but it is known as a purchase invoice, and this is checked against their original purchase order.
➤ Company A sends payment to company B.

## SALES TO PURCHASE COVER

It is important to understand this concept. You must at all times know three things:

➤ The amount of money owed to you (Debtors).
➤ The amount of money you owe (Creditors).
➤ How much you have in the bank.

Let's have a play around with this and assume your position is as follows:

Money Owed £100,000.
Money you owe £100,000
Bank £100,000

In this position, you have 1:1 cover sales to purchase, which is just about ok. But you have £100,000 in the bank, so this is acceptable.

However, had you only £10,000 in the bank, the position would be very tight indeed.

The balance of these three components must be monitored closely. It is acceptable to owe more than you are owed, but only if you have more in the bank. If this is the case, your credit controller is doing a good job.

# SKILL 40

## WORK IN PROGRESS

This is an extremely important financial concept which you really should understand, as it can be very useful, but also difficult to explain. If you struggle with the concept, I apologise in advance – email me through the website and I'll fill in any gaps.

You hopefully have a good understanding of sales and purchase and that your accounting software will have captured all the sales and purchase invoices. The creditor and debtor reports will show you instantly what you owe, and what you are owed. This information is in your accounting system, and set in stone.

However, like most things in life, there are grey areas. In business, WIP is one of those. WIP is one big grey area actually. It is very useful for a business owner to understand this concept.

WIP is the work you have ongoing in your system, that hasn't been accounted for yet.

WIP is work that has been done, but you have neither invoiced your clients, nor been invoiced by your suppliers for that work.

On a large project, this could represent a substantial amount of money.

WIP is significant, because it goes directly on or off your bottom line profit, so can have a big effect on corporation tax. WIP is virtually impossible to identify to the penny.

## HOW TO CALCULATE WIP

The calculation of WIP will vary greatly from company to company, depending on sector, size and type of service or product. In my experience, the exact calculation of WIP is near impossible, and open to interpretation, and every accountant will have their own way of calculating. I've seen two accountants lock horns over the subject for hours.

There is no right way to calculate WIP, and it will definitely never be 100% accurate. There are too many variables.

However, in order to explain the principle further, a person trying to calculate WIP could follow this sequence:

> ➤ Agree the end of the accounting period date, typically month, quarter or year.
> ➤ Calculate the value of the work complete, up to and including that date, that is not yet invoiced to the client.
> ➤ Calculate the financial value of all suppliers' work up to that date for which you have not been invoiced.
> ➤ Take one from the other, and you have the WIP.

Therefore WIP = Work complete but not invoiced, minus suppliers' work and materials complete but not invoiced.

In theory, this should be somewhere around the expected profit margin, and some accountants use this method to calculate WIP, although I don't like this method, as profit may not be as expected.

## WIP AND THE ANNUAL ACCOUNTS

WIP is shown on the balance sheet as a current asset, a short-term asset. Because it is money expected in within a year.

WIP is shown in the profit and loss account as a sale. Your WIP gets added directly to your sales. A high WIP equals more sales, more sales equals more profit, less sales equals less profit. Corporation tax is paid on the amount of profit you make. I'll leave it to you to work out the significance of this.

But I will say one thing. When I learned that I was in shock for a while, and slightly peeved. Peeved because we are fed the line that the accountancy process is thorough and exact. It is not.

Everything that is on your accounts system is exact, like I said, set in stone. But because of the complexity of calculating WIP in some companies, the accounts could be unreliable. Speak to your accountant and ask how they intend to work out your WIP, and please make sure you understand the process.

# SKILL 41

## YEAR END AND MANAGEMENT ACCOUNTS

Year-end accounts are a legal requirement and useful to a certain extent. Management accounts are not a legal requirement, but they are absolutely invaluable. You will not be able to run your business for very long without them. It'd be like swimming in the dark – you'll have no idea where you are.

As previously mentioned, I'd always try to keep your bookkeeping in-house. You can outsource, but in my experience, accountants are very busy, and you'll be waiting too long for vital information.

Also, there are times when you need to make financial decisions quickly, and you'll need the figures to hand. So, my advice is:

> ➤ Recruit a good bookkeeper.
> ➤ As soon as you can afford it, employ a management accountant to produce monthly accounts.

Initially your bookkeeper could produce management accounts for you, but it is really not a good idea in the long-run. The person who keeps the books, should not be the person who produces the accounts. It's like asking someone to audit their own work – they will seldom find anything wrong.

## YEAR-END ACCOUNTS

Year-end accounts are produced by your accountant, usually a few months after your year end. This is because there will be invoices coming in which relate to the previous financial year, and the hope is to capture as many of those as possible.

Your accounts comprise two main parts as discussed in Skill 35 and 36: the Balance Sheet, which looks at the financial performance of your company from the day you started to date, and the Profit and Loss account, which looks at the performance of your company for a financial period, month, quarter half-year or year.

Your accounts must be submitted to Companies House within nine months of your year end, to avoid fines.

Depending on the size of your company, the accounts you submit do not have to be the full P&L and balance sheet; they can be abbreviated. I would strongly advise you to instruct your accountant to submit abbreviated accounts for as long as you can, as the information shown is confidential, and your competitors would certainly benefit from your full accounts.

The information shown on abbreviated accounts allow the public, a bank or an investor to see the highlights of your balance sheet and other summarised information, but not the full breakdowns. You are allowed to submit abbreviated accounts if you are below two of the following:

> An annual turnover of no more than £10.2 million
> Assets worth no more than £5.1 million
> 50 or fewer employees on average

If you are over two of these thresholds, you will require a full audit.

Again, the audit usually happens soon after your financial year end, carried out by your accountant's auditor. He or she will come to your offices and go through your paperwork and computer accounting system with a fine-toothed comb. No stone will be left unturned.

The audit is actually designed to protect distant shareholders. To ensure that the directors have prepared financial statements honestly and fairly, acting in the company's best interests, and that accounts have been prepared in accordance with best practice and the Companies Act.

An audit can be a costly exercise. But if you are an entrepreneur, and no longer work in your business, but employ a management team, I would strongly advocate an audit for peace of mind.

Even if you are under the threshold, it is still a good idea to pay for an audit, at least every few years. It will give you an independent opinion on the quality of your accounting information.

## MANAGEMENT ACCOUNTS

The following line has a piece of advice that, if I were you, I'd really take on board.

Make sure you have monthly management accounts prepared for you.

You need to know at least this:

- ➤ Turnover
- ➤ Gross Profit
- ➤ Overheads
- ➤ WIP

The balance sheet is less important – this can wait until the year-end. But the profit and loss account (P&L) must be available to you monthly.

These are relatively simple to prepare. A P&L is shown on your accounts system at the push of a button. The management accountant will assess WIP and make manual adjustments.

These should be on your desk at the end of week three, of the following month. For example, if the month end is 31st August, the accounts should be with you by 25th September at the latest.

## HOW TO USE MANAGEMENT ACCOUNTS

The information in your management accounts is used by you or your senior team as a strategic tool, to enable you to make decisions that keep the business in the safe zone and going towards its goals.

In the first instance, the figures are compared with the predictions in your annual budget, as in Skill 42. These are the questions you ask yourself when assessing your accounts:

- ➤ Have we achieved enough turnover?
- ➤ How much gross profit have we made?
- ➤ What were overheads running at?

Management accounts give you an early warning system of problems, and enable you to take corrective action sooner rather than later.

For example, let's say you needed £1m per month turnover, and 20% gross profit to cover overheads and make profit. But for three consecutive months you only turned over £800,000.

You would need to increase turnover to more than £1.2m in the coming three months to make up the shortfall. Or if that were not possible, possibly lose some overhead, unfortunately, usually staff, which is the biggest overhead.

A result like this would certainly focus your sales and marketing activity to bring in more sales, as it would curb your spending. But at least you would know there was likely to be a problem, before it was too late.

I have found that with good management information, and quick remedial action, it is virtually impossible to go under. It's all a question of balance. Balancing turnover, with gross profit and overheads. Then comparing with and adjusting to your budget.

# SKILL 42

## PREPARING YOUR ANNUAL BUDGET

This is another essential concept. You must understand how to put-together your annual budget.

The budget is actually a predicted P&L for the year, and this becomes your financial KPI.

It works by you predicting what the following will be in the coming year:

- ➢ Overheads
- ➢ Gross profit
- ➢ Turnover

From this, the cost of sale and net profit will be calculated, as in skill 35.

This will be your financial planning document, and the management accounts will be compared against this monthly. I have found it impossible to trade without a budget.

So how do you start to put together your budget?

I always start with the things that I know to be fact, or almost fact.

## OVERHEADS

The only thing I can be almost certain of in the coming year, are my overheads. Why? Because I know what my wage bill and general outgoings are and were last month and last year, and the year before, so I know I'm not going to be far off for the coming year.

I know what my utility bills are, what my rent is, my stationery costs, IT costs and so on. All adjusted for growth (hopefully) in the coming year.

If I were starting a new company, I'd be able to work out my overheads fairly accurately. I'd know what I needed to live on and what the set-up costs were.

In short, the 'only' thing I could be fairly sure of at the start of the year, would be my overheads.

One note here. I've worked with many business consultants, and read many books that say you should start the year by predicting a turnover, and then come up with sales strategies to achieve that turnover. I remember one guy, who constantly asked me, what I was going to turn over next year. I said £10m. He said, ok, where will you get that work from? In my earlier years as an MD I bought in to this BS, until I realised that the people advising me had never actually run a business, or had done, but failed.

In my opinion, you cannot predict turnover. The only thing you can predict with reasonable accuracy, are overheads, and even they could vary throughout the year.

## GROSS PROFIT

So, there you are, you have your overhead figure for the coming year and you have divided it by twelve. Let's say overheads are £600k annually, that's £50k per month. What next?

The next question is, is there anything else about my accounts that will be similar to the previous year? The answer is GP. Why? Because you can tell from previous years' accounts and management accounts what sort of margin you were making. If your GP was in the region of 20% last year, there is no reason to believe that it won't be at the same level in the coming year.

If you are intending to operate in the same market with the same product or service, for the same clients, then there is every reason to believe GP will be similar.

With adjustments for the coming year, you can predict your GP fairly accurately.

If it's a new start-up, and you have no previous figures to work from, you'll need to assess what level of GP you think you can achieve.

The key is to work out the highest price you can charge, and still sell the product. If you can't make your business profitable at that price, then you have to look internally at efficiencies, and cut costs.

The market can be harsh – when you think you've reduced prices all you can, the market will force you to cut costs even more. You will feel, at times, as if it's impossible to reduce prices further, but I always think, if someone else can make it work for that price, so can I. All it really means is that your competitor's business is more efficient than yours.

## TURNOVER

You now have two of the three components required for your budget. Overheads and GP. The missing component is Turnover.

We can calculate the turnover you require, by asking the following question?

What turnover will I need, at 20% GP to pay my overheads of £50k per month?

This figure will be your break-even figure. See example below:

If you know your overheads are £50k per month, and GP is 20%, what turnover do you need per month to pay the overheads of £50k?

The answer is £3m in sales per annum.

£3m @ 20% = £600k
£600k /12 = £50k per month = break even turnover.

So, you must turn over at least £3m a year @ 20% GP to pay your overheads.

But you need to make money, so let's budget to turn over £4m @ 20%. How would things look then?

£4m @ 20% = £800k less overheads of £600k = £200k Net Profit (NP).

## BREAKING IT DOWN INTO MONTHLY

|              |       | YEARLY | MONTHLY |
|--------------|-------|--------|---------|
| TURNOVER     |       | £4M    | £334K   |
| COST OF SALE | @ 80% | £3.2M  | £267K   |
| GP           | @ 20% | £800K  | £67K    |
| OVERHEADS    | @ 15% | £600K  | £50K    |
| NP           | @ 5%  | £200K  | £16.6K  |

Therefore, with an overhead of £50k per month, you need to turn over £334k @ 20% to give you a 5% NP.

This is the basis of your budget. Month on month your turnover needs to be in the region of £334k with your GP at 20%.

You should now plot this out for your company for the whole year. A simple spreadsheet will suffice.

Set it out as shown above, listing all the overheads and the months of the year across the top.

I have prepared a detailed spreadsheet for your use at our book website *www.carmelcresttraining.com/50skills*

## CONTROL

Boom, as my property mentor Mark says, now you have control of your business!

You know that £50k will come out of the bank each and every month, whether you turn over any work or not. It's a scary proposition at the start of the year. You will have to pay people whether you are busy or quiet. But now you are prepared for that. £50,000 is in your head as the figure coming out of the bank monthly.

You are fully aware that month on month, you need to invoice at least £334k at a gross margin of 20%. You are aware that if you do, you will make £16.6k a month profit, and by the end of the year you'll have made £200k.

Your target is to exceed this.

You can now sleep at night. Well, if you hit your targets you can.

## MEASURE AND KEEP THE BALANCE

Now that you have the formula for success, all you need to do is monitor. Keep a month by month check on things. This is where your management accounts and KPIs come in. I set KPIs for financial performance, including turnover, GP and overhead.

Arrange for your bookkeeper to have the accounts the same day every month; make it part of their routine. Once you have the figures, compare with your budget.

Is turnover up or down? Is gross margin in the region you expect, are overheads as expected? If you are concerned about poor performance in any of the areas, look into it. It could be that an annual bill, say insurance, has been paid that month, which has outbalanced the figures. Or it could be that a big invoice went in a couple of days late.

The financial results on your monthly management accounts will vary a lot, which is fine – there are a lot of variables. But the important thing is to build up a picture month on month, and the averages should look something like your budget.

If results are worse, look into the matter, and take corrective action. If results are better, look into why, and do more of it.

One more thing, let your bookkeeper and senior managers know that they must exceed £334k per month at 20% GP. If it looks like you will not achieve this, get passionate about it, step it up and make it happen.

Only use incentive schemes if the budgeted figures are exceeded, then you can't lose.

Do all this and you will stay in business; don't do this, or something similar, and you have little chance.

I'm not going to say you've been warned again. Oh, I just did.

# PART 6:
# WHY BUSINESSES GO WRONG

I've given you all you need to get started and grow your business. Now we need to focus on you staying in business. I can't have you becoming another statistic after reading my book, can I now? That would be bad for my credibility! So here are my top tips for surviving and thriving.

As I've mentioned, most businesses go under in the first year, and the statistics are not much better right up to year five. Then things improve as the business becomes established and the owners more experienced.

It is a fact that the odds of you going out of business are more than they are of surviving. Why? Because not many people do the things I've mentioned in this book.

But, if you have read and learned from this book, your chances of survival are very much improved, and I'd like to think that if you take on board this chapter, your chances are foolproof.

These are the things I've learned can put you out of business:

> Lack of or wrong type of Insurance
> Being a technician, not a skilled business person

> ➤ Poor cash flow
> ➤ Big mistakes
> ➤ Low profit
> ➤ Not understanding peaks and troughs
> ➤ Divorce

The annoying thing about going under, is you rarely know you are. You're usually so immersed in the business you don't notice. Going under just creeps up on you, until it gets to the point that you can't pay your bills. Then it's usually too late.

Things like lack of, or wrong type of insurance, can put you out of business almost instantly, as can big financial errors. Others more slowly, such as poor cash flow or low profits. We'll discuss each of my list in turn and look at ways to get early warning.

Top of my list for good reason, isn't what you might expect – it's insurance.

# SKILL 43

## INSURANCE

Every company must carry Public Liability and Employers' Liability insurance, known as your PL & EL insurance.

Public Liability insurance covers you for a claim from the public who has suffered injury as a result of your business. It's not against the law not to have cover, but please think it as such.

Employers' Liability insurance covers you for a claim from an employee or ex-employee due to an injury suffered at work. This insurance is required by law.

Professional Indemnity insurance, PI insurance, is personal cover for professionals that offer advice, design or services. Again, it is not a legal requirement, but all professional bodies require it as standard and most clients too.

There are many other insurances you could require depending on your sector and I would strongly advise you from day one to find a good insurance broker. They will advise on the insurance you must have and the insurance you should have, and they will also suggest all sorts of weird and wonderful insurance you don't need. They get paid on commission, remember.

Also, don't just accept the first price they give you – like anything else, the cost of your premium can be negotiated. One year, I got my broker down from nearly £30k to under £20 premium, for the same cover.

You can pay your insurance up-front, but please don't – it will hit your overheads, and most brokers offer payments spread over ten months for a small amount of interest. Cash, as John Trueman says, is reality: always keep it in your bank.

I've put insurance at the top of my list of things that can put you out of business instantly, and I'd like to illustrate this with a true story of something that happened to me around three years into my business.

Two of the directors and I were travelling back from an event at the NEC Birmingham late at night, when I received a phone call from a police officer. He said a three-storey townhouse my firm had been refurbishing in Camden was on fire, and that the fire had spread to all three floors. Panic set in.

A neighbour told me later there were fire engines, police cars and a crowd of people. The house was in a bad state, and adjacent properties had been smoke damaged.

The accident had happened earlier that day, when a painter was using a blow torch to burn off old paint on a window. Something must have caught alight inside the cavity wall, and spread up and down into adjacent floors. The fire brigade said that if they hadn't been alerted when they were, the whole block would have gone up.

No one was hurt, thank god, as the place was unoccupied, but after that, my first thought was, am I insured? I didn't know if I was or not, I didn't take much interest in insurance in those days, usually leaving it to our admin person.

We drove straight to the office to check the policy, and soon realised we were not insured for hot work.

Panic really set in.

I called my broker after midnight, and he answered (that's the sort of service you want). The first thing he asked was, had the work been sub-contracted out. By chance, it had, to a local painting firm, who, it turned out, were insured for hot work. Lucky for us.

After a lot of hassle, the sub-contractor's insurer paid out more than £500k, and that was back in the early nineties.

Our premium went up massively the following year, but had we not sub-contracted the painting work, I'd probably still be paying for it today, and the company certainly wouldn't exist.

From that day I understood that insurance, and more importantly, exactly what we were insured for, was my responsibility. Delegate the task, by all means, but you have the responsibility.

Insurance, or lack of, the number one on my list of things that can put you out of business very quickly.

# SKILL 44

## THE TECHNICIAN

Michael Gerber, in his famous book The E Myth, coined the phrase "technician". The technician is a skilled professional who has trained in a particular field and become expert. Such as an accountant, or roofer. Two extremes, I know, but they can be from any trade or profession.

These people are typically high achieving in their field, and this gives them the confidence to start their own businesses.

They usually have a ready-made client base from their old contacts and do very well indeed, managing to keep prices low, due to low overheads and high quality.

Good service coupled with low price means they become busy quickly, needing to put in more hours and recruit help. Typically administration staff, or another 'one of them', to share the load, but they still continue to do what they have always done, accounts or roofing.

I've seen this situation worsen, with technicians working all hours to keep clients happy. But ultimately reliability and then relationships suffer, and sometimes ill health. It's a common theme.

What is the solution?

If you think about it, the skills required to build a business have nothing what-so-ever to do with the skills required to be a good accountant or roofer. These people are now business men and women, not employees.

We experienced this recently with a new ground-working company. I think they lasted eighteen months or so before notifying us that they were going under due to poor cash flow. Why a ground worker thought he could run a business with no training is beyond me.

If you are a technician thinking of starting a business you have two choices:

> ➢ First, learn how to run a business from someone who has done it, and then employ someone to do the technical work, your old job, while you manage the business.
> ➢ Second, partner with or employ a business manager or managing director with the required skills to run the business while you carry on accounting or roofing.

If you choose the first route, the problem is the kind of knowledge you'll need to run a business will not be available to you in any college syllabus. But you can read this and other books. So, recruiting a good MD is often the way.

Technicians put a lot of time, effort and money into their start-up, and often keep pushing through until their health or relationships suffers. This kind of business failure is sometimes tragic.

Technician, my number two. Don't let this be you.

# SKILL 45

## CASH FLOW

By now you know what cash flow is – remember the pot filling up with money in Skill 37. Poor cash flow, especially unidentified poor cash flow, can be a slower painful death.

Let me put it as simply as I can. Poor cash flow is nearly always due to one thing: inadequate credit control. It's as simple as that. People just do not get on the phone and chase debt. Or rather they don't invest the money to employ someone to do it. Employ a good credit controller, even one day a week, and your problem will disappear.

Death by poor cash flow looks like this. Your bank account will go down and down and down, with little replenishment. You will try to slow down paying suppliers – eventually they will stop supplying you. Every payroll-day will be painful, and eventually the bank with their beady eyes on your account (and they have) will identify they are at risk if they honour your payment, and they will put a hold on your account. That's game over.

Apologies for repeating myself, but it's very important you understand this point. It's simple to have great cash flow. All you have to do is:

- ➤ Employ a credit controller to manage your debts, someone good on the phone.
- ➤ Get an aged debtor report put on your desk weekly. See who owes you money and how much.
- ➤ Have a late payment process. Shout early and loud.

# SKILL 46

## MISTAKES

Another one that can put you under very quickly. Big mistakes.

There are small mistakes as in Skill 11, and that's fine. I view those as opportunities. But there are also big mistakes, which should be avoided at all costs. Especially in the early years, when there isn't perhaps the cash around to bail you out.

There have been a few occasions where I have made big mistakes. Funnily enough it has usually been me, not one of my team, who made the big ones.

I'll tell you a story that cost me millions over the years.

Our construction business works in the healthcare sector. We had a large contract for a hospital in London. The contract was an external refurbishment of the nursing home block.

During a site visit the architect told us to allow "safe access" around the building. I allowed for mobile towers at a cost of £2,500, as I deemed that to be safe access.

We were successful in our tender and during the pre-start meeting, the architect asked us what access we had allowed. I said access towers. To which he replied, "no, I want a full scaffold", as per the specification.

Somewhere in the one hundred or so pages of architect specification, it called for a full scaffold, to enable the work to be carried out safely. Now the nursing home in question was a large four-storey building, around one eighty metres long; the scaffold cost was in the region of £250,000.

There was no way we were going to accept a loss of nearly £250k, so I decided to back out, even though we were contractually committed.

I drove straight from the site to the Director of Facilities' office, walked in and introduced myself with assertiveness. It was a big gamble, but I explained the situation, and that if the Trust made us do the work, it would threaten the wellbeing of the company. I appealed to her sense of morality.

Luckily for us she had a conscience and persuaded the authority not to pursue the claim. We got away with it, but we have never worked for that trust again or any of the people who worked there, even years after. They were a major source of work and would have been for years to come.

This taught me one very big lesson in business, the old saying is true: 'the devil is in the detail'. It also taught me that if something like that happens, forget social norms, forget anything. Act quickly and decisively to put yourself back in a safe position. As the leader, you need to do things you wouldn't normally do.

If you are like me, a big picture person, and prone to skip reading, then recruit someone who loves the detail – that's where mistakes are mitigated.

So, the lesson here is clear. Put checks in your systems to ensure those sorts of mistakes can never happen. Since that day, all of our tenders are what we call 'buddied'. This means that all tenders are scrutinised with a buddy for mistakes before being sent to the client. It has saved us millions over the years, I'm sure.

# SKILL 47

## LOW PROFITS

Low profits, like poor cash flow, can kill a business slowly. Nipping away at your bank balance until eventually the bank comes knocking on your door. Having no cash is depressing, it stifles your creativity and growth, and leads to disputes with suppliers and staff. I've been there a few times, and the only way through is to dig deep and work your way out.

How can you ensure you are getting the profits you need?

Simply by early identification of profit through your accounting system.

Your accounting system must be able to run a job costing module, and identify two things:

- ➢ GP per project.
- ➢ GP for the company as a whole.

We allocate job numbers to all jobs, which is shown on our purchase orders and on all invoices we receive. Job numbers are also shown on timesheets. All costs are allocated and posted by job number, which enables us to tell instantly what we have spent, and what we have invoiced on that job.

If a project lost or made money, you need to understand why, then do more of what made you money, and correct the system that lost you money. This is absolutely vital. You must know how each project performed and which are your best and worst earners.

This whole process should form part of your month-end reporting procedure, prepared for you by your accounts people.

You must identify poor profit early, and take remedial action to protect the business.

One note on this. I agreed to take a very low margin for a prestige client years ago. I thought they would look good on our CV and we could advertise the fact to other prospective clients who may be impressed.

I was wrong. Sometimes some of the biggest names are the worst clients to work for. Don't get taken in by the lure of future work or of the prestigious client. Remember John's words, cash is reality, and a loss won't pay your overheads.

# SKILL 48

## PEAKS AND TROUGHS

Just like the ebb and flow of the waves and the changing of the seasons, there are peaks and troughs in business.

I used to get caught out a lot in the early days. When the firm was on a peak, and worse, when that peak plateaued for a few months, I'd get used to the good times and fall into the mistaken view that things were always going to be that good. Very short-sighted of me.

In a peak, there is plenty of work and money in the bank, life feels good. It's so easy to become blasé. A training course here and there, expenses, pay rises, bonuses, cars and new houses. Spend spend spend, and it all seems perfectly acceptable at the time.

Then without exception the tide turns, winter settles in, work and money dry up, to be replaced with stress and anxiety.

The problem is, you still have to pay the direct debts of goods or services you bought during the peak times. You may have given pay rises, people have gotten used to receiving large expense claims, and now you have to go back on the agreement. This causes discontent and disputes with staff, who care not about your story of woe.

Jim Rohn says, "in summer, prepare for winter". Because if winter comes and you have no food, you'll die.

I tell my sons who run our firms that in a peak, when you have plenty of money, be even more vigilant, get even more frugal, haggle for good prices even harder, and save money in a separate account.

Also, because there is plenty of money around in a peak, you, and so your bookkeeper, tend to let the financial reporting slip. This is not good – keep the continuity going; you want your accounts people on the ball ready to anticipate the signs of a trough, and you have my word, a trough will always follow a peak. The only thing that changes is the length of the plateau.

On the good side, a peak usually follows a trough, so long as you've survived the trough, that is.

So, the lesson here is like the squirrel: put away some nuts for the cold winter.

One more thing, try to prolong the peaks, and minimise the troughs.

# SKILL 49

## DIVORCE

My advice sometimes gets personal, but business is personal, and I know for a fact that divorce can ruin your firm.

Ask yourself a question. Under what circumstances would you give away half your business for nothing? No circumstances, right? But if you get divorced, the decision may not be yours to make.

I understand the circumstances of divorce may vary greatly, so I can only speak in general terms, but I can give you my experience.

My business life from age twenty-seven to thirty-nine was amazing. We were on the crest of a wave. The company grew rapidly, and won many business awards. We were held as a best-practice company by the Department of Trade and Industry, and I was invited to present here and there, including a couple of television programmes called The Learning Zone. We also made a lot of money in that period.

Then the marriage went wrong. My life between the age of forty and forty-one was very different. I moved out of my nice five bed, unencumbered marital home in the January, into a one bed flat over one of my offices. No furniture and no creature comforts, and worst of all, no children.

Without all the sordid details, the following year was a mini hell, which ended with the four boys living with me, losing my five-bed home, pensions and a heap of cash, to the now ex-wife, in court.

In one year I'd gone from high flyer to single parent of four young boys – the youngest was five, the eldest thirteen. Could I focus on the business? Not really. I was preoccupied with school runs, football weekends and cooking. My ex had done all the home making when we were married, so it was a steep learning curve for me.

I can remember driving to important meetings keeping my eye open for a fruit and veg shop to buy bananas, because I knew we were short at home. My business turned from rapid growth, to lifestyle business, and it stayed that way for the next ten years.

The first year was the worst. I'd never had to cook before, or do the washing or ironing. But I did, and so did the boys. We were a strong family of five, five blokes in a house doing the best we could.

Perhaps our closeness led to the boys, one by one, coming into the business, but that's another story. One thing I am sure of, is that the additional responsibility they had at an early age, led to their being able to accept responsibility above their years at work.

Needless to say, divorce can seriously affect your business, health and finances.

I'm no marriage counsellor, but if you've read Skill 10, you'll know that I feel your choice of partner is the most important decision you'll ever make, by far. Please choose wisely.

# BONUS SECTION

# SKILL 50

## THE GATHERING OF WEALTH

I couldn't justify putting this subject under business, as it's not really about business; it's about life choices, how you use the money you earn, and again, I'm going to reveal my past mistakes, in the hope that you won't repeat them.

As a young lad in Dagenham, life could be tough, although I didn't realise it at the time – to us it was normal. No one had ever heard of university in my school, let alone go there. But apprenticeships were plentiful, and I landed a five-year engineering apprenticeship. We all had similar lives in our ex-council homes.

I've always been good with my hands, and in my early-twenties, I started to make some money working weekends on top of working for my father. One of my private jobs was building a porch on a house in Dagenham, and with my name board outside the house, this grew, until I had a couple of friends building porches with me, taking a cut of their money. I earned more money weekends than I did during the week, and I saved that money, paying off chunks of my mortgage.

When my dad left the business in 1992, I gave myself a pay rise, and with annual profits from the company, things were really moving along for me financially. In my thirties, I was living very well indeed.

Then I lost my way a little. I started to buy cars. There's very few cars you could name I didn't own in that period. Not just one, but two or three at a time.

As luck would have it – and I call it luck, because I didn't know any better back then – I've always been frugal with money at work and at home, and I was certainly obsessed with the business, so I always had cash reserves. But looking back, the weakness was cars.

I remember one day John Trueman joking with me, when he saw yet another of my new cars, saying something like, "Well, Ray, you can either have long-term wealth, or cars; you can't have both". I laughed, but that comment struck a chord with me, and I eventually stopped buying cars.

Some years later, looking back, I realised that had I still been buying cars and not invested the money in appreciating assets, I'd still be working today, instead of the free life I have. One thing is for sure, though, I'd have achieved financial freedom a lot earlier, had I ploughed that money into property and not cars. You live and learn.

The freedom I have today is due in part to something I read in a book called, The Richest Man in Babylon, by George Samuel Clayson, written in 1926. Also to Rich Dad Poor Dad, by Robert T. Kiyosaki. Please have your children read these two books, or better still, read them to your children, as early as you can.

They are all time classic life-changing books, and they set out the golden rules of wealth.

The golden rule of wealth according to George Samuel Clayson is this:

> ➤ Work hard at any job and earn as much money as you can.
> ➤ Save some. George says 10%, I say at least 25%. Think of it like a bill, a debt to yourself that you can't touch.
> ➤ Learn to live on the balance. Trust me, you can.
> ➤ Work hard to get promoted, and earn and save more.
> ➤ When you have enough, invest the money in appreciating assets, such as property, that will also provide you with passive income.
> ➤ Repeat the process until financially free.

That's it. Amazing, isn't it, and foolproof. But very hard to do when you want to impress the opposite sex with your new convertible, or big house.

The choice is very simple.

Have it all now and be working forever, or save now and have an easier later life. By later I don't mean fifties or sixties. If you start this from college you can easily get to financial freedom by thirty-five.

The usual working-class response I get to this is, "But I don't want to give up my younger life". It makes me smile. Do they think someone who is working towards a meaningful goal is less happy than they are? What it really means is, you are working towards your dream while they are watching soaps or getting drunk.

Not very sexy, is it, giving up the new model BMW for the three-year-old Ford? But trust me when I say, if you don't do this, you'll be the one driving the Ford later in life.

I look at it like this: assuming you start to save aged sixteen, and become financially free aged thirty-five. That's nineteen years of dedication. But at thirty-five, you probably have forty-five good years left in you, plus you never have to work a whole day in your life again, if you don't want to. I'd say that's a great bargain of your time.

Also, don't forget that you will be living on the cash flow, not the principal. That will be there for your children. What a win-win.

I consider what I've just told you worth a million times this book and more.

I of course told my sons this. It was taken up with varying degrees of enthusiasm. The two younger sons have embraced it full on. The twenty-one-year-old Luke has his own buy-to-let property, and my twenty-six-year-old Adam, his own home. Alex, the sixteen-year-old, will have his before he is nineteen. They are like Ebenezer Scrooge, squirreling away their hard-earned money.

Unfortunately, I learned this myself when my elder sons Steve and Ben had already formed bad habits, like me in the early days. But they are catching on quickly, and luckily, they are great business people so they have good money earning potential.

Although I learned this in my forties, I still managed financial freedom in my mid-fifties. I can tell you that there is no better feeling on this earth than waking up knowing that you do not have to worry about money. You can literally do what you want when you want, and I am sure this is a big part of happiness.

I hope you will now consider this life changing advice and follow the advice in The Richest Man in Babylon and Rich Dad Poor Dad.

I'd like to include one more sentiment here, at the end of this book, which I hope you will take on board. I've had worries in my life, stress over the business, relationship issues and so on, like we all have. But please believe me when I say, there is no greater worry than the worry of going into old age with no money.

So, my hope is that rather than being a consumer, you will become an accumulator of wealth, and avoid that pain later in life.

# AFTERWORD

We've come to the end of 50 Skills and I'd like to thank you for reading my book. I'll leave you with what I consider to be the best advice I can give you.

First and foremost, sales. Never forget: nothing happens without work coming in, this is your – the boss's – responsibility. Make sure you prioritise it.

We discussed in Skill 28 that growth can only happen in two ways. Organic growth, where repeat work and referrals will grow the business, through maintaining a high-quality product or service. Then driven growth, from sales and marketing activity.

Much effort needs to be focussed in these areas.

At the same time, you need to have strong systems in place and measure the following:

> ➢ Make sure you have great cash flow. It's all about your credit controller.
> ➢ Make sure you are getting the gross margin you need. That's the pricing and execution of the project.
> ➢ Protect yourself from big mistakes. Build checks into your systems.

…and don't forget to get insured!

Good luck, work harder that anyone in your organisation, and set strong goals – these will pull you through the tough times.

Put the time and effort in while you are young, and save, then invest for when you are older. Become an accumulator of appreciating assets and live frugally.

Contact me through the website if you need more help.

Good luck!

**Ray Spooner**

BV - #0038 - 220219 - C0 - 229/152/17 - PB - 9781912183791